Silence on Fire

"Fire came forth from the Lord's Presence."

—Leviticus 9:24

I will try...
To be my own silence:
And this is difficult. The whole
world is secretly on fire...

...How can [one] be still or
Listen to all things burning? How can he dare
To sit with them when
All their silence
Is on fire?

—Thomas Merton,
The Strange Islands, p. 88

Silence on Fire

The Prayer of Awareness

WILLIAM H. SHANNON

CROSSROAD • NEW YORK

1991

The Crossroad Publishing Company
370 Lexington Avenue, New York, NY 10017

Printed in the United States of America
Typesetting output: T_EXSource, Houston

Library of Congress Cataloging-in-Publication Data

Shannon, William Henry, 1917–
    Silence on fire : the prayer of awareness / by William H. Shannon.
      p. cm.
    ISBN 0-8245-1076-3
    1. Spiritual life—Catholic authors. 2. Contemplation.
3. Prayer—Catholic Church. 4. Catholic Church—Doctrines.
I. Title.
BX2350.2.S435 1991
248.3—dc20   90-44037
                                                        CIP

Contents

Acknowledgments

Reprinted by permission of Farrar Straus and Giroux, Inc.:

Excerpts from *The Hidden Ground of Love: The Letters of Thomas Merton*, selected and edited by William H. Shannon. Copyright © by the Merton Legacy Trust.

Excerpts from *Love and Living* by Thomas Merton. Copyright © 1965, 1966, 1967, 1968, 1969, 1977, 1979 by the Trustees of the Merton Legacy Trust.

Excerpts from *The New Man* by Thomas Merton. Copyright © 1961 by the Abbey of Gethsemani.

Excerpts from *The Road to Joy: The Letters of Thomas Merton* selected and edited by Robert E. Daggy. Copyright © 1989 by the Merton Legacy Trust.

Excerpts from *The School of Charity: The Letters of Thomas Merton* selected and edited by Brother Patrick Hart. Copyright © 1990 by the Merton Legacy Trust.

Excerpts from *Seasons of Celebration* by Thomas Merton. Copyright © 1950, 1958, 1962, 1964, 1965 by the Abbey of Gethsemani.

Excerpts from *Seeds of Destruction* by Thomas Merton. Copyright © 1961, 1962, 1963, 1964, by the Abbey of Gethsemani.

Excerpts from *A Vow of Conversation: Journals 1964–1965* by Thomas Merton. Copyright © 1988 by the Merton Legacy Trust.

Reprinted by permission of New Directions Publishing Corporation:

Excerpts from *New Seeds of Contemplation* by Thomas Merton. Copyright © 1961 by the Abbey of Gethsemani.

Excerpt from *The Collected Poems of Thomas Merton* by Thomas Merton. Copyright © 1977 by the Merton Legacy Trust.

Excerpt from *The Asian Journal of Thomas Merton* by Thomas Merton. Copyright © 1973 by the Merton Legacy Trust.

Materials in chapter 1 appeared in modified form in *Cistercian Studies*, 25 (no. 3) 1990.

Materials from chapter 8 appeared in modified form in *The Way* (Heythrop College, London), January 1990.

THE PRAYER OF AWARENESS

"Help me to *live* in Your Presence."
—Prayer, Sixth Sunday, Ordinary Time—

"May I experience the Joy of Life
in Your Presence."
—Prayer, Seventeenth Sunday, Ordinary Time—

"I will walk
in the Presence of the Lord
in the land of the living."
—Psalm 116:8—

Introduction

This book is intended as a sequel to *Seeking the Face of God*. In that earlier work I attempted to present a pre-Reformation approach to prayer that seems to have been lost for centuries and is only now being rediscovered. Actually, it was never really lost. It survived among those who are often seen as being on the "margins" of the Church, but who time and again have been instruments of a Providence that through them calls the Church back to the center and to what is fundamental in human and Christian life. These "marginal" people I refer to are monks. This is not to say that monastic people have not had their problems keeping in tune with what is deeply central to human existence. After all monks are human beings very much like the rest of us. But it does seem that there have been moments in history when monastic figures, whether an Anthony of the desert or a St. Bernard or a Teresa of Avila, have been able to say what their times needed to hear. No one has spoken out more strongly or more eloquently in our contemporary society than the Trappist monk of Gethsemani, Thomas Merton. Speaking from the margins he has recalled our world to some of the realities of human life that are central and basic to the "good life."

One of Merton's great contributions to the contemporary world is that he has made "contemplation" a household word. At least he has done so for many people. Before he "popularized" the term (and I don't mean "popularized" in any pejorative sense; quite the contrary), most people identified contemplation with Teresa of Avila or John of the Cross or some other person of mystic qualities whom they saw completely removed from their kind of life situation. They never thought of it as having any place in their experience (except maybe to read about it in the stories of these "highly favored ones"). There are still many people who feel this way, even some who have read Merton. In their heart of hearts they want to think that he is right (that contemplation can be for them), but it sounds too good to be true; hence they are at best skeptical and at worst hostile to the whole idea. Indeed, I have had people say to me: "You shouldn't be going around giving talks and retreats that fool people into thinking that contemplation is for them. Let them content themselves with going to church and saying their prayers and keeping the commandments. They don't want to be disturbed by these new ideas about prayer. So lay off!"

Now it is possible that they may be right. Maybe I ought to be writing about the commandments and morality, since I did spend a good share of my career in academe teaching Christian ethics. But at the present time in the Roman Catholic Church that area tends to be a kind of "mined" field, in which almost anything creative you might want to say could easily hit an explosive and blow up in your face. So I prefer to "take my lumps" talking about prayer. After all, wrapped up inside any worthwhile discourse about prayer are a lot of things about morality and creative conscience and social responsibility. *No one who talks about prayer can talk just about prayer.* It impinges on so many areas of human existence. It's a kind of "Trojan horse" way of entering into discourse about morality. And these days it is a much safer (please, don't read that as "more cowardly") road to travel into that area of discourse.

Talking about prayer, though, generates its own problems: not the least of which is getting at the meaning of the word "prayer." You may have noticed that I have been slipping back and forth between the word "prayer" and the word "contemplation." And this book is actually about what I want to call the "prayer of awareness" — a term that I used in *Seeking the Face of God.*

All I really want to do in this Introduction is a bit of cleaning up of the language we use about "prayer": to take a look at the different, but related, ways in which we use the term. Thus we contrast community prayer (liturgical prayer, for instance, being one form of it) and personal prayer. Sometimes meditation or contemplation is called prayer. And there are other, more explicit, ways in which we talk about prayer. There is prayer of praise, prayer for forgiveness, intercessory prayer, and yet others. I think, though, that there is a fundamental distinction into two ways of speaking about prayer that can cover all the various activities we have customarily designated by this term. In approaching this distinction I find helpful the two Latin words that are used for "prayer," namely, *preces* and *oratio.*

Oratio, which means "discourse" or "speech" (often a well-prepared, even written-out speech) is not difficult to understand as a term for "prayer." In fact, it is quite common to think about prayer as "talk" or "conversation" with God (at times in a formal, structured way, as in liturgical prayer). *Preces*, which means "beseeching" or, perhaps better, "begging" can also assume the form of talking or conversation. But the word does have, I believe, a darker and deeper meaning. Its close relation to the word "precarious" is something of a tip-off as to that meaning: it suggests relating to God in a condition of instability, risk, total vulnerability. Those who pray are, if you will, in the constant state of existential precariousness. They are conscious of living continually on the edge of nothingness, yet equally conscious of being kept from falling into that abyss by the sustaining hand of God. This kind of prayer is "begging" not so much *at the level of words*, but, more profoundly, *at the level of being*, where there is no need to say anything and where no words would be adequate.

It is precisely in the different meanings of these two Latin words that I see two fundamental types of prayer that may be distinguished: namely, *prayer with words* and *prayer without words*. *Prayer with words* is the type of prayer with which we are perhaps more at ease and which we generally have in mind when we think of "prayer." It is so named because it puts into words the various ways in which we are able to express our *total dependence* on God. Thus, we offer *praise and thanks* to God, first for our being and then for all the gifts that go with being. But in the context of our dependence on God there is a sense of gifts misused, and so prayer may take the form of *repentance and a plea for forgiveness*. Word-prayer also looks to the present and the future, wherein we are just as dependent on God as in the past. So there is the prayer of *intercession*.

Prayer without words is not so much expressing our dependence on God, but rather experiencing it and being so overwhelmed by that experience that words become so inadequate that they are useless. Nor are they really needed. Silence alone is appropriate.

In the first part of chapter eleven of Luke's Gospel (verses 1–13), we are offered a picture of both these kinds of prayer. This Gospel passage creates a moving picture. We see Jesus at prayer — a sight that fills his disciples with awe. They are careful to respect his moment of silent, wordless communing with God. They wait. And when he has finished his prayer, they ask him: "Lord, teach us to pray." His response to their request is a discourse on prayer that begins with a model for "prayer with words": what we have come to call "The Lord's Prayer."

This plea voiced by the disciples is not just their request. It is the cry of a needy humanity knowing its dependence on God and experiencing the need to express it. And in this Gospel reading we have Jesus' response to this deep human need: first, his wordless prayer to God and, second, his gift to his disciples of "prayer with words" (the Lord's Prayer) together with an instruction on that type of prayer.

Jesus gives no instruction, however, on *wordless prayer*. Instead he gives an example of it, which they are able to see. Probably he gave no instruction on this kind of prayer, precisely because, since it is *wordless*, it is difficult to put its meaning *into words*. For prayer without words is silence: not the silence that is simply a pause between moments of noise, but a silence that is rich: filled with God, on fire with God's Presence. It is the prayer of quiet rising out of solitude in which we seek to deepen our awareness of God's Presence in our lives. It is humble, simple, lowly prayer in which we experience our total dependence on God and our *awareness* that we are in God. Wordless prayer is not an effort to "get anywhere," for we are already there (in God's Presence). It is just that we are not sufficiently conscious of our being there. We need wordless prayer to ensure that there is depth to our prayer life.

It is especially this wordless prayer that will be the subject of this book. This is the approach to prayer that I suggested almost disappeared from Church life (except in the monasteries) in the post-Reformation period. The highest degree of wordless prayer is what our tradition has called "contemplation."

This book is an attempt to clarify what I have termed "the prayer of awareness." This prayer is not quite the same as contemplation, at least not necessarily so, though that is the direction in which it is always moving. It embraces all those levels of awareness of God that — however deep they may be — fall short of that total awareness that alone deserves the name of contemplative prayer. Contemplation is a special gift of God given, not on demand, but when and as often as God wills it — though, we must add quickly, given with a marvelous largesse from a God who is never niggardly with His/Her gifts. The prayer of awareness, which is wordless prayer that opens our hearts and our persons to the Presence of God apprehended by faith, disposes us for contemplation. I would not, however, want to draw too sharp a distinction between the two; for the prayer of awareness, especially where faith is deep, is often on the borders of contemplation and, indeed, not infrequently makes forays into its territory. When, therefore, I use the term "contemplative spirituality," as I shall in the first chapter, I intend to include in that designation not only contemplation, but also its poorer but honorable relation, the prayer of awareness. In addition, when I use the word "contemplative" in the following pages, I want the reader to be able to say: "He means me." For I want to include in that term not only those who feel graced with the gift of contemplation, but also those committed to the prayer of awareness, who are on the path to contemplation and are, therefore, "contemplatives-in-process."

Wordless prayer is a kind of firm foundation for prayer with words. For without this deep awareness of God's dynamic Presence in our lives, which comes with wordless prayer, we would probably become restless and uncertain in our prayer-life (wondering whether we are doing it properly, worrying about our distractedness, etc.). With wordless prayer as the secure root of our spirituality, we shall never become overanxious (at least never for long), because we shall know that we are in God and so is all else that is. This is what really matters: all reality charged with the glory of God's Presence.

Writing a book on prayer and spirituality is an exciting experience, because there are so many people today who are searching for an authentic interior life. They want to get away from institutional squabbling and moral hair-splitting and the sometimes fundamentalist devotionalism of so much religion today and simply experience God in their lives. They want to build an inner unity that will enable them to make decisions about their lives and actions in freedom and in peace. All this is a wondrous sign of a growing maturity.

It has come none too fast in the Roman Catholic Church. In the new milieu created by the Second Vatican Council, there is no room for "spineless Catholics." And when I say "spineless," I do not mean "cowardly" but rather "unable to stand up straight on their own." To use the same metaphor, in a slightly different fashion, one could say that the Catholic community of faith can no longer tolerate "spiritual invertebrates." I borrow this somewhat curious comparison from that giant contemporary Roman Catholic theologian Yves Congar. In a charming interview, which he gave to Bernard Lauret at his hospital room in the Institution des Invalides in Paris, Congar talked about the post–Vatican II Church and his hopes for the future. At one point, speaking about the kind of Catholics whom the future will require, he quotes what he admits is a rather strange remark from the Belgian theologian Emile Mersch: "Some animals are surrounded by a shell because they have no skeleton." Taking this statement as a point of departure, Congar suggests that the highly protective structures of the post-Reformation Tridentine Church (with its ecclesial authority that brooked no questions and offered no dialogue, with its catechisms and their clearly defined doctrines and carefully spelled out moral certainties) served as a protective shell for Roman Catholics for over four hundred years. Those protective structures are fast disappearing or at least being radically modified. To quote Congar:

> Today the shell — i.e., the Tridentine system, Tridentinism — has largely dissolved, been sloughed off in some way and the need for some kind of *inner framework* has become all the more imperative. (*Fifty Years of Catholic Theology*, SCM, 1988, pp. 5–6; italics added)

Or, as he puts it in terms congenial to the theme of this book:

> Now the fate of the Church seems to me increasingly to be bound up with a spiritual and even supernatural life, that of the Christian life. *I think that in the present conditions the only Christians who can stand the pressures are those who have an inner life*. (Ibid., p. 5; italics added)

The climate in which the spiritual backbone of this inner life is discovered (or rather recovered) is the climate of prayer, especially that prayer without words, in which a Voice — deep within and inseparable from our truest self — speaks to us from the depths of our own silence, as that same Voice spoke to Moses from out the burning bush. It was when Moses was in the wordless silence of the desert that God came to him; and Moses experienced a deep and abiding sense of the divine Presence. The way God came to him changed Moses' life. For it set his silence on fire.

1

Two Approaches to Spirituality

"It Is Thou!"

One day a Lover approached the home of his Beloved. He knocked on the door. A Voice within responded to the knocking: "Who is there?" The Lover answered: "It is I." The Voice within spoke, almost sadly: "There is no room here for me and thee." The Lover went away and spent much time trying to learn the meaning of the words of his Beloved. Then one day, some time later, he once again approached the home of his Beloved and, as before, he knocked on the door. Once again, as had happened earlier, the Voice within asked: "Who is there?" This time the Lover answered: "It is Thou." And the door opened and he entered the home of his Beloved.

I begin this book, which is about wordless prayer centered around awareness of the Presence of God, with this charming Sufi story, because I think it may serve as a kind of parable that describes two different modalities of spirituality or, if you will, two schools of spirituality. Act One of the story offers a paradigm for a spirituality that is clearly dualistic. By that I mean that God and the human person are seen as clearly separate one from another. However close we may approach to God, through God's grace and our good works, God is unqualifiedly the "Other." By our very being as creatures, we are necessarily separate from God. Standing before God, we can only say: "It is I."

Act Two of our brief drama expresses a different understanding of spirituality. Its central assertion would be that, while I am distinct from God (in the sense that clearly I am not God), still I am not separate from God. Indeed, the very reality of my creaturehood means that, separated from God, I am — quite literally — nothing. In separation from God, I would simply cease to be. Hence when I become aware of God's Presence, I can only say: "It is Thou."

If the reader will indulge me, I should like to clarify these two "ways" of spirituality by telling, at a personal level, my own journey from the one school to the other. At the outset I should make clear that this shift in my way of looking at spirituality was affected and, to a great degree, even effected by my reading of the works of Thomas Merton. I trust, then, that I may be excused if along the way I quote (almost inordinately) his words, for the light they shed on my own thinking. I might sum up in very brief fashion how he influenced my spirituality by saying that, due to the impact of his writings on me, I have become quite comfortable, in saying to God, not "It is I," but "It is Thou."

I choose to make use of my story, not because I particularly want to talk about my own "spirituality," but because I think the understanding of spirituality that I had — before I came into contact, in any serious way, with the writings of Thomas Merton — was probably typical of most priests, religious, and, I would say, most sincerely committed Roman Catholic Christians of my own generation. It may also have been, allowing of course for obvious modifications, expressive of what spirituality meant for Christians other than Roman Catholics.

Spirituality of Devotion
To give it a name, I would describe the first school of spirituality, the one that directed my living of Christian faith from my earliest years, as a "spirituality of devotion." I do not intend this term disparagingly, as if it were a spirituality concerned only with externals. No, as a follower of that school I believed deeply in an "inner life," a life of grace that somehow involved a participation in the life of God; but this inner life was fostered largely by external, devotional works of piety. The problem, as I see it now, was that I gave so much attention to the activities that nourished and strengthened that life that I had little time (or at least gave little time) to reflecting on that inner life itself and what it meant. A crude way of putting it would be to say that I spent so much time trying to do the things that would please God that I had no time left just to be with God. It is fair to say that one

of the principal emphases in the spirituality of devotion was *the doing of certain things (especially devotional things) that were considered to be pleasing to God.* "Going to Mass" was considered one of these devotions that would be especially pleasing to God; and so was "going to Confession." Obviously these were the big ones.

But there were lots of other devotions too. There were, for instance the "Nine First Fridays," which many people "made" over and over again. No one seemed to think that once was enough: there always seemed to be that urge to "make them just once more," to be on the safe side. Then there were the novena people, and novenas came in all varieties. I was a "litany man" myself. I had special devotion to the Sacred Heart and used to say the litany of the Sacred Heart every day. In fact, I used to say it at Mass, while I was serving Mass. I remember how pleased my seventh grade teacher was when I told her I was doing this. It was so good, she thought, that I was managing to get both these devotions done at once: getting my Mass in and also the litany of the Sacred Heart.

And then, of course, there were the devotions of the "prayer cards." People accumulated various prayers, which they put in their prayer book and which they said every day. You could acquire quite a pile of such prayers; in fact you could get to the point where you almost resented it when someone gave you yet another prayer card — even one reputed to be especially "powerful" — because you already had so many to say and you knew you would feel a bit of guilt if you didn't add this new one to your list. The process of saying all these prayers had a name: it was called "getting my prayers in."

I don't want to poke fun at a way of spirituality that so many of us took very seriously and that is still the way of spirituality of a fair number of people. Obviously there is more to this type of spirituality than I have described above. Moreover, various types of devotions are certainly a valid, even necessary, way of approaching God. But all this being said, I still must add that it would be regrettable if we simply stopped there and did not go on to deeper ways of praying. It would also get matters completely out of perspective if we tended to treat all devotions as if they were of equal importance.

A Subtle Pelagianism?   But what I want to point out most of all is that there is, I think, behind this mode of spirituality a mentality — subtle, perhaps often unconscious — that needs to be seriously questioned. It is the tacit assumption that, if I did all these "religious things," God is most certainly bound to be pleased with me and will take good care of me. It is a kind of subtle Pelagianism (the heresy of salvation through works), which pointed out ways of winning God's good favor, of making points with God, as it were. It was as if we all started out neutral and then had to prove ourselves to God. The principal way in which we "proved ourselves" was by doing these various devotional things that for some mysterious reason — which we never questioned — God was supposed to find pleasing.

It was always a puzzle to me why nobody ever seemed to ask why it was that my "getting my prayers in" was so pleasing to God. After I became a priest (and it was in the heyday of Catholic guilt — the days of many confessions), I must say that Saturday after Saturday I got terribly wearied having people saying the same thing over and over. I found myself hoping that I might get a bank robber, maybe fresh from his holdup, the loot still with him, but wanting to get absolution as he was making his getaway, or perhaps someone who had just drowned his or her mother-in-law. And I guess I couldn't help wonder if God might not have similar wearied feelings about those same prayers "being gotten in" each day and maybe God was hoping at times that some people would be a bit more original. More like Jeremiah, for instance. Jeremiah's prayers didn't come from any prayer leaflet or prayer book. They came right out of his heart. He got angry with God and said some rather nasty things about God — right to his face. I have an idea that after hearing all the pious stuff, God, if I may put it this way, probably got a kick out of hearing what Jeremiah had to say. (I must confess, in parenthesis, that this anthropomorphic way of speaking about God — namely, as One with whom we engage in conversation, generally polite and pious, but for people like Jeremiah, often heated and reproachful — poses its own problem, which we shall discuss later when we speak about the kind of language we use in talking about God.)

A Mediated Spirituality   Returning to devotional practices, I should point out that a fair number of these devotions were directed not to God, but to favorite saints. There is a subtle theological nuance hidden there too. I remember someone saying to me: "Oh, I don't pray to God. I'm not good enough for that. I go to St. Anthony." This touches on a very deep human fear that can be found in many religions: the fear of getting too close to God. People generally find themselves more comfortable with a mediated spirituality. By that I mean a spirituality that does not reach God directly, but gets to God through the medium of certain "sacred" persons or prescribed rituals. Thus priests, ritual acts, sacraments, the saying of prayers, and the ministrations of the Church — all these can serve as intermediaries making any contact with God less scary. Remember how frightened the people of Israel were when they were in the desert and were told that God was about to approach them to enter into covenant with them. They did not want to see God, for to see God meant to die. So they turned to their leader, Moses, and they said to him: "You speak to God and then you can tell us what God wants. That's much safer — for us at least." In other words, they wanted Moses to be the mediator between God and them.

This is still the attitude of many people, though now it expresses itself no longer so much in terms of the fear that one may die, as in the conviction that any direct experience of God, any experience of God as God is in Himself/Herself, belongs to a future beyond this life. It cannot be a part of my experience in the present.

Micro-moral Tone   Devotional, mediated, my earlier spirituality also had a strong *moral tone* to it: it was directed toward doing God's will, in the "secular" activities of life, but God's will as mediated to me through authority, especially the authority of the Church. I was made to realize the need of changing my life so as to live more virtuously. In other words, my spirituality called for the biblical *metanoia*, the personal change I needed to undergo to be a true disciple of Jesus. But it was a *metanoia* of behavior. I have to add, though, that the moral tone of my spirituality tended to be concentrated on individual moral issues (like controlling my own passions and desires) rather than on social issues and the problems of the day. The spirituality I received did little to foster a sense of social responsibility. Individual in its

direction, it had little to do with community. My great task was
to save my soul.

Compartmentalized   Devotional, mediated, moral in tone,
my spiritual life tended also to be *compartmentalized*. By this I
mean that there was a sharp line of demarcation between the
things I did to foster my spiritual life and the things I had to
do in carrying out the duties of my state in life. While my spirituality helped me to carry out those duties, it was nonetheless
separate from them. In fact, at times the duties of my state in life
might interfere with my doing the things that built my spirituality; and I was often warned against too much activism that might
prevent me from saying my prayers or doing the other devotional
things that were necessary to keep the life of grace strong within
me. I lived in two realms: the sacred and the secular; and there
was never any question about which had the prior claim to my
allegiance.

Self-Conscious   It was inevitable that there should be a
kind of *self-consciousness* about this type of spirituality: a tendency
to emphasize the self and the human response to God. I had to
watch myself to make sure I was doing the things I ought to
do. It was my task to identify my gifts. I had to *discern* how I
needed to use them for the glory of God and the good of my
neighbor. The model of this spirituality was the young Samuel in
the temple, ready at all times to say: "Speak, Lord. Your servant
is listening." Or, in the context of Act One of our Sufi playlet:
"It is I. I come to do your will."

Verbal   This approach to spirituality I am describing was
strongly *verbal*. Words were very important: the words we addressed to God in prayer, the words we used to describe our
relationship with God. Time-honored phrases were preferred, because heresy lurked around the corner of the careless phrase. This
approach to spirituality tended, almost inevitably, to be quite
speculative: it found its secure moorings in the doctrines of the
Church, in accepted dogmatic theology. Thinking correctly about
God and using the right words were deep concerns. One must,
for example, be precise and accurate in expressing the relationship
between God and creation. While it sees God as the cause of the

world and also as the One who sustains it in existence and guides it by divine Providence, still this approach to spirituality is careful to avoid all ways of speaking that might imply any identification of God with the world God made or the world with God. Any such identification spelled pantheism. In addressing God, therefore, one must be aware of the distance, the abyss, that divides Creator and creature. We must acknowledge our separateness. We have to say, when we address God: "It is I."

I might sum up by saying that this spirituality — which I have called "a spirituality of devotion" — was more about *doing* than about *being*, more about behavior than about consciousness, more about doing God's will by carrying out God's commands and doing the devotional things that pleased God rather than about experiencing God as God truly is. It was clearly a spirituality of dualism that stressed the transcendence of God and God's separateness from the world and from us. Even if divine condescension allows me to achieve some kind of communion with God, I must still speak of separateness when I speak to God. I must say: "It is I."

I am sure that by now you are getting the point that I am attempting to describe a spirituality that, in many of its basic thrusts, I have abandoned. And it may well be that my freedom to describe it accurately is limited by my regret that I did not abandon it sooner. Yet, even if you see my description as something of a caricature, I do believe that those of you, whose memories are able to go back sufficient years, will recognize the chief ingredients of a spirituality that for a long time had pride of possession in the Roman Catholic Church and possibly in other churches too.

Contemplative Spirituality

It is time now to look at the second act of the little Sufi drama: the spirituality of a person who has learned to say to God: "It is Thou." I want to see this act of the drama as descriptive of a second school of spirituality that I shall call "contemplative spirituality" and that I want to identify as the spirituality that Merton lived and that I (and surely many other people besides me) came to know through contact with his writings.

This second mode of spirituality does not deny the many valuable insights of the first. It accepts the importance of devotions and the sacraments in the life of the Christian. Obviously it also accepts the truth of the transcendence of God. Yet it refuses to identify that transcendence with the vision of a God who sustains and guides the universe *from afar*. It would maintain that it is simply a misunderstanding of the transcendence of God to conceive of God as "there" and creatures as "here." On the contrary, once God chose to create, God's transcendence necessarily flowed into God's immanence.

In other words, the transcendence of God must not be conceived in these terms: there exists a whole series of beings or objects in the world; all of these objects are created, except One; and that One is God. Of course, as the uncreated One, God is the most important Object of all, but still an object whose existence we can prove and whose attributes we can describe. No! Such a view is simply false to reality. It is important that we realize that the transcendence of God excludes any notion that God is one existent among other existents. Rather, God is the Ground of all that exists. God is the immanent One, that is to say, the One who is present in all things as the Source whence they come and as the Ground in which they continue to be. God is in all and all exist because of God and in God.

Speaking to a group of contemplative nuns in December 1967, Merton said:

> We should have an *immanent* approach to prayer. God is not an Object. . . . God is Subject, a deeper "I." He is the Ground of my subjectivity. God wants to know Himself in us.

When at that same conference the question was put to him: "How can we best help people to attain union with God?" his answer was very clear: We must tell them that they are already united with God. Contemplative prayer is nothing other than "the coming into consciousness" of what is already there. We must, Merton says, "love God as our other self, that is, our truer and deeper self" (p. 10, Notes taken at the meeting).

The Two Pillars of Contemplative Spirituality

This understanding of God as *the Ground of all that is* and of contemplative prayer as *becoming conscious of what is already there* are the two pillars on which we can build our understanding of what is meant by "contemplative spirituality."

In writing to the students at Smith College in 1967 and commenting on their reading and sharing of his writings, Merton speaks of his oneness with them and says there is no greater happiness than "the happiness of being at one with everything in that *hidden ground of love* for which there can be no explanations" (*The Hidden Ground of Love*, p. 115). In a letter written about a year later (to a Dr. Weisskopf), Merton once again speaks of "the Ground of being":

> Underlying all [reality], in the deepest depths that we cannot possibly see, lies an ultimate ground in which all contradictories are united and all come out "right." For a Christian this ultimate Ground is personal, that is to say, it is a ground of freedom and love.... (Letter, April 4, 1968)

It is in this "Ground of Love," in which I am at all times, that I find my identity, my uniqueness, and my interrelatedness. Yet I can find myself and my interrelations with other people in God, *only if I am aware that I am in God's Presence*. The task of prayer, then, is to help me to achieve this conscious awareness that I am indeed in God. That is why I suggest that if the truth of God as the Ground of Love of all things is one pillar of contemplative spirituality, the other pillar is the understanding of contemplative prayer as the way of arriving at the awareness of what already is. I am in God. But I must realize it. What this means, in very practical terms, is that I don't have to worry about "getting anywhere" in prayer, because I am already there. I simply have to become *aware* of this. That is why I have chosen to describe wordless prayer that disposes us for contemplative prayer as the prayer of awareness.

It needs to be said, therefore, that we do not really become contemplatives. For we are — all of us — contemplatives in the root and ground of our being. For at the root of our being we are one with God, one with one another, one with the world in which we live. Spending time in prayer, therefore, must not be looked upon as a means of *achieving* this oneness, but of *recognizing* that it is there. Prayer does not *make* us contemplatives; rather it can make us *aware* that we truly are contemplatives, but at a level of perception we do not often achieve. Prayer, silence, and solitude are moments of grace that can awaken us to the contemplative side of our being. And we need to be awakened to it. But it is there for the awakening.

There is a Zen saying: "If you understand, things are just as they are; if you do not understand, things are just as they are." We are — all of us — contemplatives in the center of our being, in that Hidden Ground of Love. That is the way things are, whether we understand or not. But what a difference it makes when we do understand!

Intuition of Radical Dependence

If the two pillars of contemplative spirituality are (1) God as the *Ground of Love* in whom all things are and (2) *awareness of God* as the ultimate meaning of prayer, it may be said, further, that the intuition that enables us to identify and articulate those two pillars is the experience of creaturehood or of radical dependence.

Reflect for a moment on the meaning of radical dependence. If we look penetratingly into the deepest reality of things, we find that all things of themselves are — nothing. They (and "they" includes us) exist at all, only because at this deepest level we discover a Source, which is their Origin and the Ground in which they find their ongoing identity and their personal uniqueness.

It should be clear that experiencing our utter nothingness, our dependence, and experiencing God as the Ground of our being are not two intuitions, but one. The very experience of my dependence is simultaneously an experience of the God on whom I totally depend. Awareness of God and of God's Being becomes a light that reveals to me my own nothingness. I see only God in me. I am no longer there. I am able at last to voice the password of contemplative spirituality: "It is Thou."

Nondualism

What I need to make very clear at this point is that I am talking about *nondualism*. I am saying that God and I (as also the rest of reality) are not separate. I am distinct from God, for obviously I am not God. But I am not separate, for apart from God I am nothing. This is true of all created reality. While the world is not *identified* with God, nonetheless, it must be said that it finds its *identity*, its whole reality, in God.

One way of clarifying this point is to think of one of the favorite analogies we use to describe prayer. We often liken it to *conversation with a friend*. Think of such a conversation: you are speaking with your friend. The two of you are together in your home chatting with one another. At a certain point your friend takes leave of you to keep another appointment. After her departure, there is only you. Where before there were two in the room (you and your friend), now there is only one: and that is you.

When we use this analogy to understand prayer, we have to be very clear how analogies are intended to work in our mental world. When we use analogy we are saying that two realities being compared are alike in some respects, but different in other respects. When we use the analogy of friendly conversation as an analogy to describe prayer, we are, therefore, saying that the two are partly similar and partly dissimilar. They are similar in that in both cases there is personal encounter: in the one case between me and my friend; in the other between me and God. But we must not forget that analogy also implies dissimilarity. Thus when I engage in a friendly conversation there are two persons involved who are spatially separated one from another; I am in one chair, my friend is in another. But when I pray there is no separation between me and God. For I cannot be separated, even for an instant, from God who is the Ground of being in whom alone I find my being, my identity, my uniqueness. Thus the equation of friendly conversation might be expressed: I plus my friend equal two. But the equation of prayer would have to be: God plus me equals, not two, but one.

Once this fact begins to sink into my consciousness, there follows a realization that, at first thought, is utterly shattering, namely, that I minus God equals zero. For, were the Ground of my being to be withdrawn, I would simply cease to be. This means that I cannot conceive of myself as apart from God. Apart from God, I simply do not exist. I am not there.

But if this intuition is at first thought "shattering," it becomes, on deeper reflection, positively exhilarating, when I come to realize that the converse must also be true: if I exist, I must exist in God. Where I am God is, or, more properly, I am where God is. There is no place else where I could be. This I become alive to in prayer.

To sum up, then, the two poles of contemplative spirituality are God as the Ground of Love and prayer as awareness of this.

They flow from a fundamental human intuition of being totally and radically dependent on God.

This contemplative school of spirituality tends to be *less verbal* and less speculative than devotional spirituality. Its preference is for silence instead of words, for experience rather than scholastic terminology. It is not content to talk about the meeting of the creature with God; it wants to experience the Presence of God. While realizing the importance of being as clear as possible in speaking about God, this school of spirituality is not hung up on verbal exactitude. For it acknowledges the inadequacy of any human words to convey the mystery of God and God's involvement in all of reality. A contemplative who has experienced God and found his/her identity in God can easily empathize with the cryptic words of Meister Eckhart: "One who speaks about the Trinity lies!"

The contemplative spirituality that I am attempting to describe would also find quite congenial to its understanding of prayer the words of St. Anthony of the desert: "We pray best when we don't even know that we are praying." There is an *un-self-consciousness* that is characteristic of this way of looking at prayer. If prayer means "meeting" God, the contemplative's thoughts are on God rather than self. It is enough to know that my true self cannot be apart from God. On January 2, 1966, Merton wrote to a Sufi friend in Pakistan, Abdul Aziz, about this un-self-consciousness in prayer. Describing his own prayer he says:

> There is in my heart this great thirst to recognize totally the nothingness of all that is not God. My prayer is then a kind of praise rising up out of the center of Nothing and Silence. If I am still present "myself," this I recognize as an obstacle about which I can do nothing unless He Himself removes the obstacle. He can then make the Nothingness into a total clarity. If He does not will, then the Nothingness seems to itself to be an object and remains an obstacle. Such is my ordinary way of prayer. It is not thinking about anything, but a direct seeking of the Face of the Invisible, which cannot be found unless we become lost in Him who is Invisible.

In contemplation, it is in forgetting myself that I find God and discover my true self in God. *Since my true identity is in God*, I can indeed say: "It is Thou."

Change of Consciousness   Contemplative spirituality would
agree with the devotional school of spirituality in saying that constant change or conversion, the biblical reality of *metanoia*, is a
necessary imperative of the spiritual life. But whereas devotional
spirituality would want to think of such change primarily in terms
of behavior, contemplative spirituality, without being unmindful
of this kind of change, would tend to stress the need for a change
in consciousness. *It is not enough that we behave better; we must
come to see reality differently.* We must learn to see the depths of
things, not just reality at a superficial level. This especially means
we need to see the nonseparateness of the world from God and
the oneness of all reality in God: the Hidden Ground of Love
in all that is. Prayer is a kind of corrective lens that does away
with the distorted view of reality that, for some mysterious reason, seems to be my normal vision, and enables me to see what
is as it really is.

Two Concluding Points   There are two final points I need
to make about contemplative spirituality. The first point is concerned with what this kind of spirituality *does* to us. It is not
enough to know what contemplation and prayer of awareness
mean; we need to know also where they *lead us*. I can answer that
very simply: they lead us to all our sisters and brothers. Merton's
own story may serve as an example. In 1941 he entered the Abbey
of Gethsemani with a firm resolve to leave the world irrevocably.
He had come to seek God and God alone. What he found, as
time went on, was that his search for God was inevitably leading
him to people. And of course this is the simple logic of a contemplative view of reality. For if I am one with God, so are all
of my sisters and brothers. The contemplative finds the Ground
of Love in all reality. This is what Merton means when he says
that contemplation is "an awakening to the Real within all that
is real" (*New Seeds of Contemplation*, p. 3).

It was this nondualistic experience of God — an experience
of God as really distinct from the world but not separate — that
eventually brought Merton to the realization that "leaving the
world" is at best a metaphor and at worst an illusion. In finding
God Merton found the rest of reality and especially he found his
fellow men and women; and he discovered them, not as a face-
less mass, but as individual persons, each distinct and unique in

the eyes of God, all bound together in a network of interlocking relationships, and each finding his/her identity and uniqueness in God Who is for all the Hidden Ground of Love. This is what human personhood meant to Merton and what it must mean to us: the discovery of our oneness with our brothers and sisters in God. When we come to realize our dependence on God and also the dependence of all reality on God, we experience a sense of interdependence with all God's people, and at the same time the responsibility we have toward them. True contemplation inevitably creates a social consciousness. I must reach beyond the moral problems that engage me individually and become involved in the social issues confronting men and women of my day and age. I cannot really be aware of God if I am not at the same time aware of my sisters and brothers. For they, like me, are — in God.

Thus, when I find the One, I find the Many: my sisters and brothers; and I know that I have to be in solidarity with them in dealing with the problems that face all of us in our time in history. In a letter to Sr. Emmanuel, a cloistered nun in Brazil (January 16, 1962) Merton expressed the need for this kind of solidarity:

> [The problems of our times] are very great...People seem exhausted with the labor of coping with the complications of this world in which we live. Yet it is absolutely necessary that we do so. We have got to take responsibility for it, we have got to solve the problems of our own countries, while at the same time recognizing our higher responsibility to the whole human race.

This does not mean in any way a questioning of his contemplative calling. Instead it is a deeper affirmation of that calling. He goes on in this letter.

> And yet I remain a contemplative. I do not think there is a contradiction, for I think at least some contemplatives must try to understand the providential events of the day. God works in history, therefore a contemplative who has no sense of history, no sense of historical responsibility, is not fully a Christian contemplative....

One final point I need to make about contemplative spirituality. Commitment to such a spiritual path leads us to the realization that the whole notion of "having a spirituality" can be a dangerous illusion. My spirituality is not a separate compartment of my life but is that very life itself. We understand what Merton meant when he wrote to Etta Gullick that he objected to setting off prayer from the rest of our existence, as if we were sometimes spiritual, sometimes not. He says to her: "From the moment that I obey God in everything, where is my spiritual life? It is gone out the window" (January 18, 1963, *The Hidden Ground of Love*, p. 357).

Just as we must see that spirituality is not something we *have* as a part of our lives, but something we *are*, something we live, so more and more we need to realize that we shall come to understand contemplative prayer, not through words, but through experience. In 1966 Thomas Merton wrote:

> I don't really want to write about "spiritual things."...I have gradually developed a nausea about talking about [contemplation]. Except when I really have to. The words sound too empty and trivial. I just don't feel like spinning out a lot of words about God and prayer. I feel in fact immensely poor and fallible, but I don't worry about it. I just live. (*School of Charity*, p. 323)

"I just live." These three brief words may well sum up all that I have been trying to say about contemplative spirituality. We just live — in God and with awareness that we are in God's Presence. We approach God in confident love with three other brief words: "It is Thou." These two verbal trinities ("I just live" and "it is Thou") produce different sounds, but their meaning is the same.

2

Living in the Presence of God

"Help me to live in Your Presence."
(Prayer, Sixth Sunday of Ordinary Time)

In recent years more and more people have come to see the necessity of making a retreat, at least annually. They come to put their lives in order, to deepen their life of prayer, to achieve in their lives a sense of peace and tranquility that otherwise seems just unattainable. Different people might express their motives for coming to retreat in a variety of ways. Someone might say: "I'm going on retreat, because I need to get away, in order that I may be with God." Or another might say: "I just have to remove myself from the daily routine of my life so that I can get rid of all that distracts me and truly find God in my life."

You know how cigarette packages have to carry the warning: "The surgeon-general has determined that cigarettes are dangerous for your health." If one could put a label on retreat attitudes, then attitudes that define a retreat as "getting away in order to *be with God*" ought to carry a faith-warning, which might read something like this: "Your spiritual director has determined that such an attitude toward a retreat is dangerous for your spiritual health."

Why do I say this? Because this attitude — namely, that I must get away in order to *be* with God — embodies a belief in what might be called "spiritual apartheid"; and acceptance of spiritual apartheid is destructive of any in-depth spirituality. What do I mean by "spiritual apartheid"? According to my brand new *Dictionary of Etymology*, "apartheid" derives from the Dutch. It means: "apart-hood." "Hood" is a suffix that we sometimes add to words. It means "condition of." Thus we speak of "saint-hood," which means the "condition of being a saint." "Apart-hood" means the "condition of being apart." It is the condition in which one group of people is set apart from another. In South Africa, of course, it means whites being set apart from blacks.

When I speak of "spiritual apartheid," I mean the mentality that sets God apart from creation. God is There, created things are Here. *Political* apartheid restricts black people's presence to certain places. *Spiritual* apartheid restricts God's Presence to certain places. We have always been taught that God is everywhere, but so often our attitudes seem to belie our belief in that teaching. To say that you come to a retreat in order to be with God is to suggest that God is THERE (i.e., at the retreat house), but God is not HERE (and by "Here" I mean your home, the place where you work, the place where you go to meet your friends) or, at the very least, God is more THERE than HERE.

Spiritual apartheid is very dangerous for our spiritual health, for it tends to *limit* spirituality: restricting it to certain "holy" places and "sacred" times. As a matter of fact, there is a whole school of spirituality built on this type of thinking. You find examples of it in such a highly praised classic as *The Imitation of Christ*. The author of the *Imitation* says somewhere that he approves of Seneca's words: "As often as I go among men [sic], I come home less a man." One can't help wondering: if this is true, what kind of people was the author of the *Imitation* associating with?

This type of spirituality enshrines a mentality that would think that I am "spiritual" only on certain occasions and that most of the time I am not. It is a mentality that tends to *privatize* spirituality, suggesting that it has nothing to do with social involvement, that is to say, with realities that are not "spiritual." Thus it even places restrictions on God, because, for all practical purposes, it allows God to have meaning in only one area of our lives, namely, the area that we call "spiritual." *Political* apartheid is a grave social evil, for it separates people from one another. *Spiritual* apartheid is an even greater evil, for it separates God from God's creation and from God's people.

So we must issue dire warnings to those who say that they are going to a retreat center in order *to be* with God. For that seems to suggest that they weren't really able to be with God yesterday and the day before. Make it very clear to them that their family and their friends, who had no thought of making a retreat, are just as much in the Presence of God as they are. Moreover make it clear to them that when they get to the retreat center, they will be no more in God's Presence than they had been when they were still at home. And — something that may really give them pause — tell them that they will be no more in the Presence of God when they finish this retreat than they had been before they started.

Of course it is only fair to them that you add an important clarification. While it is true that they will not *be* in the Presence of God any more at the end of this retreat than they are when they begin, still they have every right to hope that the ending of the retreat will mean that they have become more fully *aware* that they are in the Presence of God.

This, as I suggested in chapter 1, is our great spiritual need: *to be truly aware that we are in the Presence of God.* It is, as I have pointed out, one of the two pillars of contemplative spirituality. Everything that exists must of necessity *be* in the Presence of God, but only God's human creatures are able to *be aware* that they are in the Presence of God. Trees give glory to God simply by *being* what God made them, but they are not aware that they are giving glory to God. Nonrational creatures obey God's will — again simply by being what God made them. "Snails obey the will of God — slowly." We are able to give glory to God *knowingly*. We can do God's will by choice. For we alone have the marvelous capacity, properly human, of being able to be *aware* of God.

Unfortunately so many of us do not actualize this capability: we are not *aware* that we are in the Presence of God. We are, as I say, victims of spiritual apartheid. We have the notion that generally we are apart from God, except for important moments — like moments of liturgy and prayer when we are truly in his Presence and do try to be aware that we are in the Holy Presence. That is why some people start their prayer by saying: "Let us place ourselves in the Presence of God." As if you could be any place else — except in the Presence of God. The really gigantic feat would be trying to place yourselves outside the Presence of God. If you could do it — which actually you can't — it would mean immediate annihilation for you. It wouldn't mean you would die. It would mean that you would entirely cease to be.

This is why I have been insisting that we need to realize the difference between *being in the Presence of God* and *being alive to that fact*. Being in the Presence of God is the necessary condition of our existence. God is the *Source* of my being and the *Ground* of my existence which enables me to continue in being. In other words, being in the Presence of God is not something I choose, as if I were to say: "Today I will be in the Presence of God." Or, "today I want to set aside an hour of my day and during that hour I will be in the Presence of God." No, being in God's Presence is not a matter of choice. It is not, for example, like saying: "I think I will go visit my mother today. I will be with her for tea this afternoon."

Being in the Presence of God is qualitatively different from being in the presence of any one else. For there is no one else who is essential to my existence. A lover given, as all true lovers are, to exaggeration, might say to her beloved: "I can't live without you. I can't exist without you." But *this is a romantic statement, not an ontological one*. However difficult it might be, the lover *can* exist without the beloved. For, though her existence may be very closely linked with his, she is not dependent on him for that existence. The Only One I literally cannot live without, indeed exist without, is God.

Let me suggest an example. We often think of the Christian life as a journey and, using the analogy of friendship, we think of God as one who travels with us, who walks alongside of us. Let's reflect a bit on this analogy. Think of a concrete situation. One day you are out walking and you meet a friend and you begin walking together, chatting with one another as you go along. Then at a certain point in your walk, you come to an intersection. You bid goodbye to one another; and your friend goes to the left and you go to the right. You had been walking together; now the point of separation has come. You end your walking together: each of you goes your separate way.

Now apply this analogy to God. Think analogically of your relation to God as a walking with God. You walk together, somewhat like the disciples walking with Jesus on the road to Emmaus. There is conversation (that is, prayer) as you walk along. Suppose you come to an intersection and God turns to the right and you go to the left, in the sense that you take separate paths. You are no longer, then, in God's Presence. Supposing this were a possibility (which it is not), what would happen? Put simply and starkly, you would walk instantaneously not really to the left, but into nothingness. For separate from God, we simply are not. We do not exist. We are nothing.

I remember reading a few months ago a brief news item about a town in Arizona: a tiny town, a place of less than a hundred inhabitants. With self-effacing modesty, these people had named their town "Nothing." One day a fire completely destroyed the town. The news headline describing the fire read: "Nothing is left of 'Nothing.'" If we were to be separated from God even for an instant, that would be our story: "Nothing would be left of nothing."

Being in the Presence of God, therefore, is in no sense a problem that we have to deal with in our spiritual life. It isn't something we have to achieve. For it is already and always there: it is the essential condition that goes with being a creature. What very often *is* a problem for us is that we are not sufficiently *aware* that we are in the Presence of God.

Meaning of Awareness   It is one thing to emphasize the importance of being aware of God, quite another thing to be clear about what this actually means. Awareness of the Presence of God (and I might say that "attentiveness" to that Presence or "being awakened" to it or "being alive" to it are all valuable synonyms) cannot be reduced to some particular action that we perform, though there are actions that may stimulate that awareness in us. But *awareness of God*, at its deepest level, is not so much something we *do* but something we *are*.

This point is of capital importance, because one of the things we *do* in relating to God is "to think about" God. Thinking about God and reflecting about God's Presence are important spiritual exercises; and we need to engage in them. But they are not to be confused with what we are talking about in this chapter, namely, *awareness of God's Presence*. To be aware of something does not mean to be thinking about it. When I use the word "awareness," I have in mind something very personal: an experience that in some way tends to be unitive. Thinking, on the other hand (whether about God or about anything else), tends to divide: it implies a subject thinking and an object that is thought about. Awareness or attentiveness is a very different experience. A *true sense* of awareness reduces the distance between me and what I am aware of. A *very deep sense* of attentive awareness *closes the gap* between me and that of which I am aware. It brings us together. It unites.

This is an important distinction. For I am going to say that the Scriptures tell us that we ought to be aware of God at all times, at least in a general way. If you get the idea that I am saying that you ought to be thinking about God at all times, this would pose a real problem. It could even cause some serious accidents or personal rifts. Dietrich Bonhoeffer once said that a man ought not to be thinking of God when he is making love to his wife. As a celibate priest, I shall have to take this as vicarious information. But we get the point he is making. Yet a husband who makes love to his wife can do this in the context of a sense that they are both in the Presence of God.

Thus, one can *think* about awareness of God or *talk* about it or *hear* about it or *write* about it. One can *pray* for awareness of God. But none of these is *actual awareness* of God. For in each of these instances (thinking, talking, hearing, writing) you are doing something, some specific act. But, as I have said, awareness is not something we *do*, but rather something we *are*. Someone once said to me: "I try to be aware of God, but I don't seem able *to do it*." Of course not. Awareness is not doing, but being: being with something or someone. It means communion, oneness. In fact, in a deep experience of attentive awareness, the subject-object dichotomy disappears. I am not aware *of something*. I am *simply aware*.

Let me offer an analogy that may prove helpful. Think of a professional singer making plans for a concert performance. There is a big difference between what she does in preparation for the concert and what she does at the actual performance. In her preparation she will have to do a good bit of thinking: about the music and its notation, about her voice and the way she will use it, about the text and the emotions it evokes and probably about a lot of things I don't even know about. There is a subject, the singer, and an object, the music; and the two are separate. She may also do some talking with her singing coach. She may even say a prayer or two. But all this must take place before the performance. As the performance approaches, the distance between subject and object lessens. Finally, when the performance takes place, the singer, if she is a good artist, will not be thinking of any of these things (the music, her voice, her feelings). She will quite literally become lost in her singing. It will not then be a case of a singer plus a performance. In a sense she will no longer be there: she will be one with the music. There will be pure Song.

In a somewhat similar way, there will be times in our lives when we will *think about* God: in reading, in study, and in prayer with words. But the time comes when we will want to pass beyond all this and give ourselves to wordless prayer in which there will not be the subject nor the awareness of an object possessed by a subject. There will simply be pure awareness, pure prayer. To return to the analogy of music again: it is, in the words of T. S. Eliot, "the music heard so deeply/That it is not heard at all, but you are the music,/While the music lasts" ("The Dry Salvages").

I believe that this pure awareness, this simple attentiveness, where there is neither subject nor object is what Thomas Merton means by "contemplation." Writing in *New Seeds of Contemplation*, he says:

> In the depths of contemplative prayer there seems to be no division between subject and object and there is no reason to make any statement about God or about oneself. HE IS and this reality absorbs everything else. (*New Seeds of Contemplation*, p. 167)

Three Levels of Awareness   This attentiveness, in which we discover our oneness with God and in God with all reality, may be thought of in at least three different, though related, ways. There is, in the first place, *the most fundamental type of attentiveness or awareness*: an awareness built into us so to speak. It is part of the package of being a creature. It is of the very necessity of our existence that we *be* in God; for apart from the Source and Ground of my being, I am nothing. This deep *ontological* awareness is buried within us. Many people do not know it is there. It belongs to the unconscious or superconscious level of our being; and many people never get in touch with that level of their being. And it really is a pity that we do not. As Merton wrote to a friend in England: "All that is best in us is either unconscious or superconscious" (*The Hidden Ground of Love*, p. 341).

There is a delightful Sufi story that can perhaps concretize our understanding of this deep awareness of God buried in the deepest recesses of our being. According to the story, before creating the world, God said to Adam: "Am I not your God who created you?" Adam answered: "Yes." Ever after, according to the Sufi tale, there has been in every woman and man this question: "Am I not your God who created you?" This is the silent question that is "built into" all of us: a question that calls us to acknowledge our creaturehood, our emptiness, our nothingness. The question is a prod to attentive awareness. God is there. God made us. God is our Creator: the Source of our being. And God goes on creating: God is, therefore, that ever present (though hidden) Ground that makes it possible for us to continue in being. That is why this question is created into me: "Am I not your God who created you?"

But we are created, not only with this question, but also with the answer: "Yes!" Our acknowledgment that God created us is not so much a "Yes" that we *speak*, but a "Yes" that we *are*. It too is "built into" us, whether we are aware of it or not. It is the speech of our deepest Silence.

Conscious Awareness   This ontological awareness of God (this contemplative dimension of our being, if you will), which is "built into" us, is present even if we never advert to it. It lies asleep in us, as it were, until it is awakened and we arrive at a *second kind of awareness*: conscious awareness. This is the meaning of contemplative prayer and, in varying degrees, of the prayer of awareness: to bring to the surface of our lives this fundamental awareness that is an essential element of our being. Contemplation is "waking up," it is "coming alive" to this most important reality of my existence. In moments of silent, quiet, emptying prayer, this awareness may surface in my life and I experience this awareness of God — which is at the same time an awareness of myself and all things else in God. Again, I must repeat, it is not an awareness of any Object or objects. It is simply pure awareness.

This, I think, is what Thomas Merton had in mind when he wrote in *New Seeds of Contemplation*:

> It is as if in creating us God asked a question, and in awakening us to contemplation he answered the question, so that the contemplative is at the same time the question and the answer.
> (p. 3)

Contemplation is the silent hearing of this question "Am I not your God who created you?" and the silent answering: "Yes," but with the acute awareness that the question and the "Yes" must be understood, not as something we hear and say, but *something we are*. The question and the answer put me squarely in God. Apart from God I am not an answer; I am not even a question. I am nothing.

But we must not lose sight of the point that attentive awareness of God in no sense means that I, as a separate subject, am aware of God as an object. For I as a separate subject simply do not exist. Nor can God ever be conceived of as an object, even as an object of thought and reflection. As soon as we try to grasp God in our thought and reflection (that is, as soon as we make God the Object of our thought and reflection) God disappears from our consciousness. What replaces our consciousness of God's Presence is the construct of our thoughts and words: not God, but what we think or say about God.

Thus, as I have pointed out earlier, it would be wrong to think of God as one existent Object among other existent objects or even as the Greatest Object among such a series of existent objects. God is the Source whence all reality comes. God is the Ground in which they continue to be. God is in all and all exist because of God. It is because God is Source and Ground of all that awareness of God is not awareness of an Object. It is pure awareness, simple attentiveness. Merton writes in *New Seeds of Contemplation*:

> There is "no such thing" as God because God is neither a "what" nor a "thing" but a pure "Who." He is the "Thou" before whom our inmost "I" springs into awareness [and love. He is the living God, Yahwe, "I AM," who calls us into being out of nothingness, so that we stand before Him made in His image and reflecting His infinite being in our littleness and reply: "I am." And so with St. Paul we awaken to the paradox that beyond our natural being we have a higher being "in Christ" which makes us as if we were not and as if He alone, were in us...] (*New Seeds of Contemplation*, p. 13. The section in brackets was added by Merton to the French text. Unpublished letter to Marie Tadie, November 22, 1962)

It may be said, therefore, that in contemplation I discover my true self. For the true self, whether in hiddenness or in conscious awareness, is always there: my being springing out of God Who is Being. I am distinct from God (I obviously am not God), yet I am not separate from God (for how could a being be separate from its very Ground?). Nor am I separate from all the rest of reality that also finds its Ground in God. The happiness, then, of the true self is "the happiness of being at one with everything in that Hidden Ground of Love for which there are no explanations." That "at-oneness" with everything is experienced not statically, but dynamically, in the intercourse of love that flows through everything: the love that rises out of that Hidden Ground that is All in all.

The goal of any true spirituality, therefore, is to *make us aware* — aware not only of God but of ourselves and of the great wide world of people and things. Becoming aware is really an *awakening*: we are roused from the sleep of spiritual apartheid and we become truly *alive*.

This *conscious* awareness of God, which we may experience in wordless prayer, is a gift, just as the fundamental *ontological* awareness is gift. We can open ourselves to receive it. We can strive to develop an aptitude for it: this is the precise meaning of the prayer of awareness. But this *conscious* awareness, when it comes, is always unearned, always gift. It can happen at any time, for God can give gifts when God chooses. And I really believe that many people have this gift of such unitive experiences. Sometimes we don't recognize them for what they are: experiences of God's Presence in us and in all reality or, if you will, of us in God and all reality in God. These moments of such deep experience do not necessarily come at the time we may have set aside for prayer: they may very well come when we are in the midst of people or in the shade of nature's beauty. But even if they come *outside of prayer*, I think it can be said, generally speaking at least, that they come *because of prayer*.

General Awareness   Besides these two ways of thinking about awareness (namely, the *fundamental awareness* that is the ontological condition of our being and the focused, specific, *conscious* awareness (which occurs in contemplation and, at times, in the prayer of awareness) there is, I believe, a third way of viewing our attentiveness to the Presence of God. This is what might be called a *general* awareness of God that flows from our prayer and becomes an element of the way we live our lives. We go about our tasks and responsibilities. We are not necessarily adverting in a conscious way to God (for there are other things to which we have to give our conscious attention), but there is a kind of general pervasive sense that we are in God's Presence at all times. Indeed, there may be times — though it may be only for a flashing moment — when I do actually advert to being in the Presence of God. This sense of God's Presence may be likened to the "sense of one another" that a young (or older) couple very much in love may experience. There is a kind of pervading feeling of being with one another, even when they are busily engaged in some task that requires their close attention.

This kind of general awareness of God — that may occasionally surface — is what makes it possible for us to follow Paul's admonition: "Pray always" (see 1 Thess. 5:17). If to "pray always" means "always to be thinking" about God, then "praying always" would be an impossibility; it might even be dangerous (for instance, if one were driving on the L.A. Freeway). But if "praying always" means a kind of "atmosphere" in my life, in which there is this unadverted-to realization of a Presence in which I know I am always immersed, then "praying always" becomes a distinct possibility.

On March 27, 1968, Thomas Merton responded to a Carmelite superior who had questioned him about the meaning of "continual prayer." He tells her that this is indeed a long tradition about prayer — one that goes back to the desert fathers. Yet he is at pains to point out that it is often misunderstood. It becomes a serious problem when people think it means that one must continually concentrate on some concept or some object or some feeling. "What is really meant," he says, "is continual openness to God, attentiveness, listening, disposability, etc." He continues, in words that show the obvious influence of Zen on his understanding of his own tradition of spirituality:

> In terms of Zen, it is not awareness *of* but simple awareness. So that if one deliberately cultivates a distinct consciousness *of* anything, any object, one tends to frustrate one's objectives — or God's objectives. If one just thinks of it in terms of loving God all the time in whatever way is most spontaneous and simple, then perhaps the error can be avoided. (Unpublished letter to Mother Mary Therese)

I want to conclude this chapter by offering the reader the first of three short prayers that speak of the Presence of God and that are more or less central to the message of this book: *Help me to live in Your Presence.* Note the verb: we do not pray: help me to *be* in your Presence. We don't need help with that, for — as we have seen — being in God is the very condition of our existence. We are always in God, whether we are aware of it or not.

Repeating this prayer — often — can be most fruitful. For it is *awareness* of being in God's Presence that changes our lives. The goal of our prayer, therefore, is to become aware of the divine Presence and continually to deepen that awareness. Deepening our awareness of the Holy Presence means that we shall come to *live* in that Presence with greater attentiveness during the whole of our day.

A FOOTNOTE TO CHAPTER TWO:
AN EXERCISE IN WORDLESS PRAYER
(or PRAYER OF AWARENESS)

I offer this Footnote, because people have asked me to be concrete and specific about the "prayer of awareness," but I need to own up to some misgivings in writing it. The source of my discomfort is the concern lest I give the impression that I am offering a *method* for wordless prayer. This is far from my intent. These are simply one person's suggestions that others may use if they find them helpful. Our prayer should be spontaneous and loving, not rigid and overly formalized. Each of us (at least those of us who feel drawn to this kind of prayer) has to learn the "way" he or she finds most comfortable. With this proviso, and fortifying what I say with several valuable quotations from Thomas Merton, I make the following suggestions:

1. Find a time — fifteen minutes to a half hour and at a regular time each day, if possible — during which you can be silent and quiet. (Sometimes such an atmosphere may not be entirely possible and we simply do the best we can.)

2. In order to quiet the mind and heart, take a few deep breaths, inhaling the air that is fresh and clear and exhaling the musty and the stale. Then say one (or all) of the brief prayers given

at the beginning of this book, for instance, the one discussed in this chapter: "Help me to *live* in Your Presence."

3. Gently but firmly let go of words and thoughts (even those about God), also of cares, concerns, and anxieties (at least for this brief period of time).

4. Try just to be quiet, knowing in faith that you are in the Presence of God, which means being in the Presence of Love. Just relax in the silence of that Presence. Just be there. Do not feel that there is anything you have to do.

5. If you are distracted (as surely you will be), quietly let go of the distractions to the degree that you can. If they remain or return, don't be disturbed; for you are still in the Presence of God. To deal with the distractions, you might want to repeat one of the three short prayers or some other aspiration in order to help you return to inner quiet and silence. But don't fuss too much about distraction.

6. Conclude with the Lord's Prayer or a favorite psalm or some spontaneous words of praise and thanks.

7. Try to develop the habit of saying at different times during the day one of the three "prayers of awareness" or some other aspiration as a way of keeping "awareness of God" closer to the surface of consciousness.

SELECTED MERTON TEXTS

Those who have progressed a certain distance in the interior life not only do not need to make systematic meditations, but rather profit by abandoning them in favor of a simple and peaceful affective prayer, without fuss, without noise, without much speech, and with no more than one or two favorite ideas or mysteries, to which they return in a more or less general and indistinct manner each time they pray.

The main thing is to establish contact with God by loving faith. This implies at least enough awareness for the mind to be alive to the Presence of God....

—*What Are These Wounds?* (1950), p. 95

About prayer: have you a garden or somewhere that you can walk in, by yourself? Take half an hour or fifteen minutes a day and just walk up and down among the flowerbeds.... Do not try to think about anything in particular and when thoughts about work, etc. come to you, do not try to push them out by main force, but see if you can't drop them just by relaxing your mind. Do this because you "are praying" and because our Lord is with you. But if thoughts about work will not go away, accept them idly and without too much eagerness with the intention of letting our Lord reveal His will to you through these thoughts...

—to Sr. Therese Lentfoehr, August 28, 1949
The Road to Joy, p. 195

There is an absolute need for the solitary, bare, dark, beyond-concept, beyond-thought, beyond-feeling type of prayer. Not of course for everybody. But unless that dimension is there in the Church somewhere, the whole caboodle lacks life and light and intelligence. It is a kind of hidden secret, unknown stabilizer, and a compass too. About this I have no hesitations and no doubts, because it is my vocation; about one's vocation, after it has been tested and continues to be tested, one can say in humility that he knows. Knows what? That it is willed by God, insofar as in it one feels the hand of God pressing down on him. Unmistakably...

—to Daniel J. Berrigan, March 10, 1962,
The Hidden Ground of Love, p. 73

[I] have a very simple way of prayer. It is centered entirely on attention to the presence of God and to His will and His love.... That is to say that it is centered on faith by which alone we can know the presence of God.... There is in my heart this great thirst to recognize totally the nothingness of all that is not God. My prayer is then a kind of praise rising up out of the center of Nothing and Silence. If I am still present "myself," this I recognize as an obstacle about which I can do nothing unless He Himself removes the obstacle. If He wills He can then make the Nothingness into a total clarity. If He does not will, then the Nothingness seems to itself to be an object and remains an obstacle.... [My prayer] is not "thinking about" anything, but a direct seeking of the Face of the Invisible, which cannot be found unless we become lost in Him who is Invisible.

—to Abdul Aziz, January 2, 1966
The Hidden Ground of Love, pp. 63–64

3

Experiencing the Joy
of God's Presence

"May I experience the Joy of Life in Your Presence."
(Prayer, Seventeenth Sunday of Ordinary Time)

In this chapter I want to take our reflection on prayer to yet another level. Having moved from "being" in God's Presence to
"living" in God's Presence (at least as a goal), I want to suggest
that we attempt another step: that we go beyond "being" and
"awareness" to the *joy* we should experience in being in the Presence of God. To this end I offer you, dear reader, the second of
the three one-sentence prayers that appear at the beginning of the
book: "May I experience the Joy of Life in Your Presence."

I probably should begin by saying that initially I had trouble
with this prayer. When I first noted it in the liturgy and saw its
pertinence to the life of prayer, I made a copy of it to use in
my own prayer. But very soon I had mixed feelings about saying
it. I felt it should be true: that I *should*, above all, experience
joy living in God's Presence. At the same time I wasn't at all
sure that I could say that prayer with honesty. For I really wasn't
certain that I was experiencing joy from living in the Presence
of God. My problem was that I seemed able to think of quite a
lot of experiences, which seemed to have no connection with the
Presence of God, that brought joy into my life. I enjoy writing.
It seemed to me that I might have to say that I took more joy
in writing about the Presence of God than in experiencing that
Presence itself. Then I thought of other joys in my life. I take joy
in experiencing the presence of my friends. I take joy in reading
a good book or going to a good party or counseling someone in
need or in preaching a good homily. I take joy in experiencing a

good meal or a good drink or watching a good movie or a baseball game or listening to a symphony.

But if I were pushed to list the various joys I experienced in life in some kind of hierarchical order, I wasn't at all sure that I would put experiencing God at the top of the list. I certainly felt that it belonged there. At the same time I felt I had to be honest and say what was *actually going on* in my life rather than say what I thought *should be going on*, but really wasn't.

So I kind of choked over the prayer as I said it. Yet I continued saying it, hoping that perhaps continual repetition might make it so. Remember the old song: "Wishing will make it so. Just keep on wishing and cares will go." In this case, instead of "cares will go," I wanted it to be "the joy will come."

That repetition did not make my concern about where God fitted on my list of priorities go away. What it did do, though, was to move me to reflect more deeply on some important questions, like: what does it mean to experience God? And: how could this be seen as the great joy of one's life? My reflection eventually led me to the third chapter of Exodus that finally opened up a whole new way of understanding what it might mean to take joy in the Presence of God.

Exodus, Chapter Three

This is one of the most important sections in the Bible — this chapter 3 of Exodus — for directing our thinking about God. It is all about a deep experience of God that one man had — an experience that was to become central to understanding the biblical story. Remember it is about Moses and how in the desert, one day (or maybe better one night) he sees a bush that is burning. It is different from any other bush. For it is not consumed by the fire. It keeps on burning like a kind of eternal flame. Out of this bush, Moses hears a Voice. The Voice, claiming to be that of the God of Abraham and Sarah, Isaac and Rebecca, Jacob and Rachel, calls Moses to the impossible task of leading God's people out of slavery into freedom. Moses is terrified and, knowing that the people will want to know who the God is who sent him, dares to ask the divine name.

The answer given by the Voice is four Hebrew consonants. Because the Jews after the exile did not pronounce the Holy Name and because the Hebrew language has no written vowels, the vowels that go with these four consonants have been forgotten in the dim past of history. Some have pronounced it *Jehovah*, which is almost certainly incorrect; others, *Yahweh*, which is little more than a guess. This is the reason why most translations of the Bible (the Jerusalem Bible is an unfortunate exception) simply render the four consonants as *Lord* (though even this, seen as exclusive language, creates its own problems).

The Meaning of the Holy Name

But what is more important than the pronunciation is the meaning of the word. Just as we don't know the exact pronunciation of the word, so the meaning remains obscure. Most scholars do believe that it has something to do with *God's Presence*. And, of course, this intrigued me very much, as I was wrestling with the meaning of the prayer: "May I experience the Joy of Life in Your Presence." Could the divine Name, I asked myself, provide a clue to the meaning of this prayer for me?

Western scholars, faithful to this notion that the Divine Name has to do with Presence, but drawing on scholastic philosophy instead of Hebrew remembrances, have taken it to mean God's *ontological* Presence and have translated it as *"I am Who am."* This can scarcely be what was intended. The Voice of God was not speaking to a philosopher, but to an unlettered nomad.

It is far more likely, in the light of the whole biblical context, that the name refers to God's Presence as a *Saving Presence*: a Presence that brings Salvation, Freedom, and New Life to God's people. Martin Buber has suggested that, as the name was spoken to Moses, it meant: "I will be present to you in the impending crisis that is about to take place in Egypt." And you will remember that what happened in Egypt was that God *saved* the people from slavery and brought them to freedom. And after leading them out of Egypt, God went ahead of them as a cloud by day and a pillar of fire by night. The cloud and the pillar of fire were signs of the Presence of the God who saves.

But as time went on, Israel gradually forgot that initial meeting with God, which should have told them that God is always present as a saving God. They came to feel that there were times when God was *not* a saving God. Hence later Israel posed the question: "How can I know that God is present in my life in a saving way?" The answer they developed was naively simple. It said: "You know that God is present in your life in a saving way, if things go well with you. If things go badly for you, you can be sure God is not present in your life." Put in starkest terms, this attitude says: "God's Presence is identified by prosperity; God's absence by adversity."

This is the mentality generally found in the Hebrew Scriptures. It is a recurring theme in the psalms. There are signs, however, in the Hebrew Scriptures that not everyone was satisfied with this solution. For it was a solution that seemed to belie the facts. The book of the Hebrew Scriptures that most dramatically dissents from this orthodox position is the book of *Job*: the story of a man who is thoroughly good but who still suffers great adversity. Yet despite the questioning of Job and others, this mentality persisted and was very much alive in Jesus' time; and, even though Jesus explicitly rejected it, his followers through the centuries have been all too ready to accept it. Yet the question still persists: "If God's name means *Presence* and if that Presence is not just any kind of Presence, but a *Saving* One: how can I know that God is present in my life in a saving way, as a "*Saving* Presence"? And there is also that further question to wrestle with: "Is God always present in a saving way or are there times when our God is not a "Saving God"? It is questions of this sort that constitute the stuff of what we call "religion." This is really what the religion of Israel is all about. This is what any religion is all about. This is what Christianity is all about.

For all religions have as their principal concern the question of salvation. (This is what distinguishes religion from philosophy.) The question that peers out from the pages of the sacred books of most religions is the question: "How do we find a saving God?" Or, as I have put it, in the light of Exodus 3 and the subsequent experience of the people of Israel: "How do we know that God is present in our lives as a Saving Presence?" And the further, more ominous, question: "Is God sometimes present in a way that is *not saving?*"

We have seen the answer that came out of the earliest experience of the nation of Israel and we have seen the answer of a later Israel. The Christian answer is deceptively simple. First God is *always present* as a *Saving God*. Second, There is only one sign of God's Saving Presence and that is the *experience of being saved*.

The Meaning of Saving Presence

This means that the fundamental religious question that we have to put to ourselves is this: Do we have the experience of being saved? To that question I want to say an emphatic Yes. I want to say that we all are continually undergoing the "experience of being saved." First of all, let us think of salvation in the most radical sense possible. Apart from God, we are absolutely nothing. It is only because we are in God's Presence that we are preserved moment to moment from falling into the abyss of nothingness. Every second of our lives, therefore, we are being saved by God: saved from annihilation, extinction, nothingness. In the very fact of existing at all we are experiencing God's Saving Presence.

I want to tell you that this realization — that God's Presence is a Saving Presence that I experience simply in the joy that comes from existing as a human person — was for me an enlightenment that was truly liberating. It made me understand better the prayer: "May I experience the Joy of Life in Your Presence." It enabled me to say the prayer without wondering any longer whether I might be a phony in saying it. For I could see that all the joys I had in life, however great or small they might be, existed only because of this most radical joy that came from the fact that I had been blessed with the grace of existence — a grace that could not *be* apart from the Presence of God.

In the previous pages I have tried to suggest the importance of being aware of God's Presence. At this point I am trying to push our reflections a bit further and deeper, in order that we may discover the *meaning* of that Presence of which we should be aware. So far I have tried to point out that it is not a static Presence (as if God were just there. Period.), but it is a *Saving Presence* and that this Saving Presence is seen especially in the fact that from moment to moment God saves me from extinction.

But we need to go further and realize that besides this most basic way of saving me, there are many other ways in which God is continually saving me. Not just from annihilation, but from sin and stupidity, from possessiveness and acquisitiveness. Not of course that we do not put up a fight at times to hang on to our sinfulness and greed and self-seeking. But God is ever there calling, encouraging, and waiting.

If we really believe that God's Presence is always a Saving Presence, then we come to know that when we reach out to others in unconditional love, we are being saved. When we tear down walls and build bridges in our relationships, we are being saved. When we seek our true selves in the depths of our being in God, we are being saved. When we replace a mere collective being together with true community, we are truly experiencing ourselves as being saved. And this experience of being saved is the only way we can experience God's Presence as a Saving Presence. We find a Saving God in the experience of being saved.

Indeed, whatever brings true joy into our lives — making friends and making love, being a writer, a singer, a dancer, a husband, a wife, carrying out a liturgical role as priest, lector, or other minister, doing a good job at my work, cooking a good meal, walking, jogging, swimming, using the gifts we have, and so many other things in which we take delight — are, or can be, aspects of that experience of "being saved." We take joy in these experiences and we are able to say with confidence the prayer: "May I experience the Joy of Life in Your Presence." For we understand that that is what we are really doing.

But if we are truly to have this experience of joy, we must heed the warning I sounded when I spoke about spiritual apartheid, that "apart-hood" that tries to set up divisions in our lives and tell us what is "spiritual" and what is not. We must not allow this spiritual apartheid to make us think that there are some areas of our lives that relate to salvation and other areas that have nothing to do with it. Especially we need to avoid the attitude that, if we enjoy it, it probably is unrelated to salvation; and if it's hard, it may well have something to do with salvation. Or worse still, the attitude that if it's a "sacred" object or action, it has something to do with salvation; but if it's a "secular" object or action, it probably doesn't have anything to do with salvation. Or the mentality that if it's done in church, it probably has to do with our salvation, but if it is done at home or at work, it probably doesn't.

In the April 22, 1989, issue of *America*, there is an article by Mitch Finley, a Catholic layman who writes occasional books and frequent articles for mostly Catholic publications. This *America* article is entitled "Confessions of a Modern Catholic Layman." One of the things he says is particularly pertinent to what we are discussing. He writes:

My most fundamental religious experiences do not happen in church. Rather they happen in the context of my marriage and family. . . . My spouse and children channel God's grace to me more often than do the liturgy or other church institutions. In other words my experience bears out the ancient Christian conviction (reaffirmed in the Second Vatican Council's "Pastoral Constitution on the Church in the Modern World" and "Dogmatic Constitution on the Church") that family life is an authentic form of ecclesial life.

Finley is telling us that, generally speaking, he experiences the joy of God's Presence more in what we are accustomed to call the "secular" than he does in what we have come to refer to as the "sacred." His is a strong warning against a spiritual apartheid that would find God's Presence only in church and not in God's world, especially in the world of family and friendship. It is a needed warning, because we have so long been brought up with this sharp cleavage between the "secular" and the "sacred."

Recently when I was on vacation, I stopped into a parish church, where it was evident that preparations were being made for a parish mission. I chanced to pick up a copy of the prayer that people had been invited to say for the success of the mission. The prayer seemed to be more a sermon cast in the genre of a prayer. By that I mean it seemed to be speaking not so much to God as to parishioners who may have been on the fence about making the mission or who may even have decided not to make it.

It starts out with a description of what a good parishioner ought to be:

> Almighty God
> I want to come closer to you,
> I want to love you more dearly,
> Hear you more clearly
> And follow you more nearly.

Then comes the examination of "parishioner's" conscience: chiefly in terms of the busyness of his/her life that might tempt him/her to miss the mission and thus depart from the ideals expressed in the first part of the prayer. And of course all along "parishioner" knows that all these elements of busyness are just excuses and that one could, if he or she really tried, take the time to add the parish mission to an admittedly busy life.

> I find my life so busy, Lord,
> That's why I find it so hard
> to take out time just for You.
> You know all the excuses I have:
> Responsibilities to my family,
> My work, my health, my need to relax.
> There are so many things I have to do
> That I am hesitant to add one more thing.

Should "parishioner" then decide that it would be wiser to skip the mission this year? Maybe wait till next year when he/she may not be so busy? By no means! That choice is not seen as an option at all. What "parishioner" must do is to ask for the strength, which only God can give, to put his/her life in perspective: so that "I can let go of the things that hold me back." And the prayer ends as all prayers should with a word of thanks to God; in this case it is thanks for all the good that "parishioner" will receive from the mission: "help me to reap the full benefit of our mission." Whatever had been "parishioner's" state of mind when he/she started the prayer, the prayer ends, so to speak, with its "mission" accomplished. "Parishioner" has asked for the full benefits that can come from the mission — which means that he/she has made the choice to go.

A prayer of this kind is not only a transparent example of clerical "blackmail": conniving to trick "parishioner" into making the parish mission and enlisting God as an accomplice in the conniving; it is also the stereotype of spiritual apartheid. It comes close to saying: "God will be at the mission. That is where you will find God's Presence. So don't let anything interfere with this opportunity of being in that holy Presence." Again, there is the strong suggestion that "secular" activities, such as earning a living, caring for one's health, and other worldly things, have nothing directly to do with hearing God, loving God and doing God's will. At best all these things are neutral and when set over against the parish mission can be obstacles to spiritual growth, if "parishioner" chooses them over it. Such a mentality divides human life. It separates the sacred from the secular. It separates God from much of creation.

Salvation and This Life

There is another form of spiritual apartheid that needs to be mentioned. I refer to the mentality that would think of salvation as something that is purely eschatological, that is as a reality that is experienced only after death. To be saved is to achieve a blissful life after death. It is to be in heaven. This attitude, which suggests that salvation occurs only *after our leaving* this world, comes dangerously close to implying that we are in reality being saved *from* the world. Or at best it may mean that what we do in this world can help us on the road to salvation; but that real salvation does not take place here.

Such a mentality would conflict with the biblical understanding, for in the Bible "salvation" has the character of wholeness, completeness. This would mean that, while it is true that we attain perfect wholeness only in the life to come, nonetheless everything that contributes here and now to our wholeness and well-being, to our total health if you will, may be seen as "experiences of being saved" and, therefore, indications of the ongoing "Saving Presence" of our God.

Always a Saving Presence?

Realizing that God is for us always a Saving Presence must surely be a source of great joy for us. It can make it quite comfortable, as well as very meaningful, for us to say the prayer: "May I experience the Joy of Life in Your Presence."

But there is yet one problem we must deal with before we can be perfectly comfortable in the saying of this prayer. I have said that God is always a *Saving Presence* for us. There are many who do not believe this. They would point to the terrible evils that exist in our world: the destructive powers that are sometimes experienced from the forces of nature, in tornadoes or hurricanes or forest fires and, even more significantly, the inexplicable injustices that exist in our world: the exploitation of the poor and the marginalized in society, the frightful inequalities in our society based on race or color or sex. How does one find the Saving Presence of God in the midst of such gigantic and powerful evil?

I'm sure you are sitting on the edge of your chairs eagerly

awaiting an answer to this question. Sorry, but I have to squirm a bit and finally say that this is a question that admits of no easy answer. Evil is a huge mystery and intertwined with the mystery of evil is the mystery of human freedom and God's respect for that freedom. This is too large a topic to enter into here. But we can, I think, sidestep it for now and try to understand why, despite these mysteries, the very reality of God demands that God's Presence must always be a Saving Presence. God is the Hidden Ground of Being for everything that is. But that Ground is not an abstraction, much less an intellectual construct. The Ground that gives being and subsistence to all that is (including the highest beings of all, namely, persons) must be personal. The word we use to describe personal giving is "Love." God is, therefore, the Hidden Ground of Love; or, to put it in the language of John's first epistle: "God is Love."

We shall be reflecting on this description at greater length in chapter 7. For the present I simply want to place our understanding of God's Presence as a Saving Presence in the context of God as Love. One thing this means is that there is something that you and I can do that God cannot do, that is, not love. God cannot look at one of us and say: "Oh, yes, there is a person who is obviously unlovable. I shall withhold my love from her." I can say that. You can say that. But God cannot say that. For the God whom Jesus has revealed to us — in striking ways different from the God of the Hebrew Bible — is a God of unconditional Love. Love does not flow from God to us because God sees something in us that moves Him/Her to love us. No, love flows from God because of what God is in Himself/Herself: God is Love.

This is why I say that God's very Being demands that God's Presence be a Saving Presence. God is always present to save. Another way of putting this is to say that God does not punish. Our sinfulness or sometimes evil ways may bring hurt to us, but this is not punishment from God. For God's love for us does not depend on what we do but on who God is.

In a recent issue of the *London Tablet*, a very popular feature writer, John F. X. Harriott, wrote a column called "Bully for Guilt." In it he took to task a religious affairs correspondent on the BBC, who said that she "was a bit depressed at the guilt that still lingers for [people] with Catholic backgrounds." Harriott spoke in rather glowing terms of the constructive value of a "healthy guilt." To quote him briefly, in snatches:

> I consider my time better spent feeling guilty about offending Almighty God than the editors of *Harpers & Queen*; fretting over my state of grace than my expanding waistline; and weighing the prospects of eternal bliss rather than an extra year or two of cheerless old age. What is more I know whose company I prefer. Those hoary old Catholic sinners, pickled in whiskey and twinkling with lechery, rooted like oaks in the faith, manfully owning up to their sins and trusting in the mercy of God....
>
> Bully, I say, for Catholic guilt. It has made high drama of millions of modest lives.... It has launched more good novels than Helen's face did ships. It inhibits all kinds of wickedness.... The Chinese leaders and sundry other despots would be vastly improved by a good strong dose, not to mention the evil-doers nearer home. It is those who feel no guilt whom we should really fear. Feeling guilt is a grace, a rich organic manure, just the thing for healthy growth. Let us be loud in its praise and sing in chorus: we may be guilty, but we're feeling fine. (July 1, 1989)

In the very next issue of the *Tablet*, letters to the editor (one of the best features of the *Tablet*) took him severely to task. I quote just one letter:

> I was brought up in the pre–Vatican II Church where guilt was all-pervading. Even as a six year old I can remember being too frightened to go to sleep in case I died in the night and went to hell. Guilt did not make "high drama of millions of modest lives"; it made misery of them.... We heard little of the loving relationship between the creator and his children; a lot more about what would happen if we disobeyed the rules or if we died on the way to confession. (July 8, 1989)

All too many people of the pre-Vatican II era of the twentieth century could, I am afraid, identify with that letter and with something of the bitterness it embodies. It remains a sad period in the history of the Church — one that we trust will not be repeated. It was not an era in which to take joy in the Presence of God — at least for most people.

It is difficult to see how such a state of affairs could have risen in the first place. It was a denial of the God revealed by Jesus

Christ, the God who *is* Love and, therefore, whose *Presence* is always a *Saving* Presence.

Understanding God as Love means that we must banish forever the notion that God ever deals with us in a hurtful way. This understanding can also take us a big step toward deepening our perception of what it is we are talking about when we refer to contemplation and to the prayer of awareness. Thus far we have struggled through two basic truths. The first is that we are always in the Presence of God (and can be "nowhere" else); the second is that prayer (especially wordless prayer) is being aware, being conscious, of that Presence. Now we are in a position to take our thinking a bit further: if God is Love, then, "our always being in the Presence of God" can be reexpressed as "always being in Love," and our understanding of (wordless) prayer as "awareness of the Holy Presence" can be refined as "awareness of Love."

"To be in love" is a familiar expression in our vocabulary. We speak of a young couple as "being madly in love" with one another. Such a term can express any number of different realities: from ardent affection to a deep and unselfish concern and commitment to one another. But such a situation can change. Two people who are in love may grow more deeply into that love or they may grow out of that love. Just as there is falling in love, so there can be a falling out of love. But when we talk of our "involvement" with God, there is no possibility of our "falling out of Love." Since we are talking about the Love that is the very condition of our existence, to "fall out of Love," would mean falling out of existence. It would mean ceasing to be. To be God's creature is to *be* always *in Love*. To pray is to *be aware* that one is always *in Love*.

I invite you to reflect on the saving character of the Holy Presence, always with the realization that it is the Presence of Love, and to say quietly, deeply, and often the prayer: "May I experience the Joy of Life in Your Presence."

4

From Awareness of God
to Awareness of People

*"I will walk in the Presence of the Lord
in the land of the living.
(Psalm 116:8)*

Would you be shocked if I were to say to you: "Only God matters;
apart from God nothing else matters"? Would you, on hearing
such a statement, be inclined to say to me: "How can you be
so cruel? My family matters. My friends matter. My job matters.
People suffering throughout the world matter. The poor matter.
How can you possibly say of the poor and of my family and
friends and of my work and of so many good things that they
don't matter?"

If you *were* shocked by my saying this and were getting ready
to burn the book in indignant protest, I would simply assert
(probably with a certain degree of smugness) that your attitude
betrays the sad fact that spiritual apartheid had struck again. For
such thinking would be proof that you are thinking of God as
apart from His/Her creation. You would be thinking that, when
I said, "Only God matters," I was also saying that your family,
your friends, and indeed all the good things of creation don't
really matter. But that isn't what I was saying at all. I was saying
that "apart from God nothing else matters." But I don't want
to think of all these good things (family, friends, etc.) as being
"apart from God." For, as I have been insisting, nothing exists
apart from God. For God is the Hidden Ground of Love in which
all reality finds its being, its identity, its uniqueness. Once God
chose to create, it became impossible to think of God without
thinking of all of us and of all of reality.

Thus I was not saying that all the things you hold dear don't matter. Rather what I was intending to imply, in the light of what I have already said, is that all those things matter precisely because they are in God. Apart from God they don't matter, for apart from God they do not even exist.

The Tendency to Make God an "Object"

What is at the heart of our problem in rejecting spiritual apartheid is the strong tendency we have — a tendency I have already mentioned — to think of God as an Object: an Object we can think about, talk about, believe in, and pray to. When we think of God as an Object, then we compare God to "other objects" and we think that true contemplative prayer means preferring God to all these "other objects." Thomas Merton has a passage in his recently published journal, *A Vow of Conversation*, that is pertinent.

Writing on his fiftieth birthday, January 31, 1965, he reflects on

> the unutterable confusion of those who think that God is a mental object and that to "love God alone" is to exclude all other objects and concentrate on this one! Fatal. Yet that is why so many misunderstand the meaning of contemplation and solitude...."
> (P. 142).

We do not turn away from the world to find God; it is rather that in finding God we discover our world in a whole new way. True contemplation involves a *total emptiness* (i.e., being empty of all separateness) and a *total fullness* (being at one with the Source and Ground of all things and at one with everything else in that Hidden Ground).

I would like to expand on this intuition of Merton's by using a quotation (which I briefly alluded to in chapter 1) from a letter Merton wrote to Amiya Chakravarty and the students of Smith College in Northampton, Massachusetts.

The background of the letter is helpful in understanding Merton's words. In the spring term of 1967, Amiya Chakravarty, a Hindu scholar and a friend of Merton, was teaching at Smith College. One of the projects he set for himself was to organize a Merton Evening for students and faculty. It was held on March

28, 1967, and involved readings and discussions of some of Merton's writings. They read selections of the poetry, excerpts from *The Seven Storey Mountain*, from *Raids on the Unspeakable*, from the *The Wisdom of the Desert*, and from Merton's book on Gandhi. The day following this brief symposium, Dr. Chakravarty wrote to Merton. He assured Merton that he had been mindful of Merton's warning not to turn such a session into a personality cult. Still, he went on to say:

> We do respond to the greatness of a person. Such greatness is an open door leading us all to the source and center of divine truth. . . . We were immersed in the silence and eloquence of your thoughts and writings. . . . The young scholars here realize that the absolute rootedness of your faith makes you free to understand other faiths. Your books have the rock-like inner strength, . . . which can challenge violence and untruth wherever they may appear. (*The Hidden Ground of Love*, p. 115)

Several of the "young scholars" also wrote to Merton telling him how pleased they had been with that evening's experience.

On April 13 Merton replied to Dr. Chakravarty and the students. Nothing can be more rewarding to a writer, he told them, than to be understood and appreciated. He expressed his belief that they had indeed understood what he had written. But more than that they had come to see something most precious — and most available too: namely, "the reality that is present to us and in us." While we may give different names to that reality (Being, *Atman*, *Pneuma*, Silence), still, however we name it, the simple fact is that

> by being attentive, by learning to listen (or recovering the natural capacity to listen which cannot be learned any more than breathing), we can find ourselves engulfed in such happiness that it cannot be explained; the happiness of being at one with everything in that hidden ground of Love for which there can be no explanations.

This brief statement is of decisive importance in grasping the contemplative understanding of reality. Merton is speaking about "happiness" and makes clear his conviction that this sum of human blessings can be found only by going beyond the dualities of life: an enormously difficult undertaking, because these dualities seem so real to us. Merton *locates* true happiness in "being at one" with everything. And that oneness is no pantheistic or impersonal experience, for it springs from a "hidden ground"; and that "Ground" is personal, for it is the "Ground of Love."

This happiness cannot be *explained*; nor can the Hidden Ground of Love in which it is to be found. But it can be *achieved* by attentiveness, by listening. For most of us, Merton seems to be suggesting, "listening" — which should be as natural to us as breathing — is in fact something we have to discover in ourselves or, rather, recover (for it is always there).

What Merton is telling us is that, when we discover God — not our ideas or someone else's idea of God, but *the living God*, the God who is beyond words and thoughts and ideas — we experience the joy of being in God and, because we are in God, we experience the joy of "being at one with everything." And this oneness is not something anonymous and impersonal, but involves the deepest possible communication with God and with our sisters and brothers.

It was about this "communication" that Thomas Merton spoke on October 23, 1968, to a group of religious leaders gathered in Calcutta. He said:

> The deepest level of communication is not communication, but communion. It is wordless. It is beyond words, and it is beyond speech, and it is beyond concept. Not that we discover a new unity. We discover an older unity. My dear brothers [and sisters], we are already one. But we imagine that we are not. And what we have to recover is our original unity. What we have to be is what we are. (*The Asian Journal*, p. 308)

The Living God

This experience of oneness comes, I have suggested, when we become aware of the *living God*: not of a God whom we have constructed in our minds, with our thoughts and ideas, or a God whom some theologian has constructed for us, but truly the "living God." There is an interesting statement about the "living God" in the Epistle to the Hebrews — a statement that a would-be contemplative ought to keep in mind. The author writes: "It is a fearful thing to fall into the hands of the living God." It is so easy to be content to live with a God who is not really "alive": a God who is an abstraction or a God whom we approach only at times of worship — and even then generally through an intermediary. Indeed, sometimes our God may be no more than a projection of our needs, our fears, or our desires. In genuine contemplation (and also in moments at least of the prayer of awareness) one meets the *living God*, bare-handed, with no gloves on, so to speak. The experience can be fearful, even dangerous. For it turns our world inside out and upside down. It transforms our consciousness and forces us to see reality in a new and totally different light. It makes us see reality as God sees it. It takes us beneath or beyond the superficial consciousness that knows only seeming separateness, alienation, manipulation, and dehumanizing of people. It sees what so many cannot see, namely, that *"being at one"* of all things in the Hidden Ground of Love. In terms of persons it enables us to see "the whole Christ," the "cosmic Christ," if you will. In experiencing this wondrous reality — that all men and women are linked together with one another in interlocking relationships that make them truly one — we are really experiencing (in a Christian context, at least) what St. Paul means when he speaks of "being in Christ."

Contemplation — Ongoing Dimension of Life

When wordless prayer has been carefully adhered to as a daily reality in our lives, inevitably (perhaps even inexplicably) something quite unexpected begins to happen in our lives. What happens is that prayer ceases to be simply (I almost want to say it ceases to be "primarily") a prayer-exercise and becomes an ongoing dimension in one's life. It's not anymore just something we *do* at certain times; it is something we *are* habitually. We begin to live our life in conscious awareness of this "at-oneness" of all things. Because wordless prayer has become a way of life for us, we are able to say with the psalmist: "I will walk in the Presence of the Lord in the land of the living."

We have finally come to the third of our one-sentence prayers, which are found at the beginning of the book, the one from Psalm 116: "I will walk in the Presence of the Lord in the land of the living." Note how the prayer has three parts. First, there is reference to the journey: "I will walk." No matter how tuned in we may be to the contemplative vision of reality, we all have yet a long way to go on this journey from superficial reality to ultimate reality, from dualism to nondualism. Now and again we catch glimpses of the "at-oneness" of all things in God. But, for much of the way, it is a faith-journey, on which we travel so often in darkness and with gratitude for the light when it comes.

For what faith assures us is that we *walk* "in the Presence of the Lord." And that Presence is a dynamic Presence. It's not just that God is there. God is doing things *to* us, *in* us, and *through* us. God is day after day saving us and, at the same time, calling us to share in the task of saving our sisters and brothers. We are saved and we save. And all this takes place "in the land of the living."

Living in Today's World   This final phrase of our prayer puts us squarely in the middle of our world. And when I say in our world, I mean the world of men and women and things as they exist now. The world of Perestroika and Glasnost, the world of Solidarity and Tiananmen Square, a world in which there is poverty and hunger, terrorism, drug traffic and injustice, a world of sexism and racism, a world in which a few are very rich and millions are without food and shelter, a world that longs for peace, yet has lived for more than four decades under the shadow of nuclear annihilation. This is our world, though we did not choose it. Though we may not have been responsible for creating these evils "in the land of the living," yet we must assume responsibility for dealing with them.

Writing in *Commonweal* in 1966, Merton said:

> That I should have been born in 1915, that I should be the contemporary of Auschwitz, Hiroshima, Viet Nam and the Watts riots, are things about which I was not first consulted. Yet they are also events in which, whether I like it or not, I am deeply and personally involved.

He goes on to explain that when we speak of the "world" we need to see it as a place of human activity, where all sorts of human motivations — some honest and decent, others devious and deceitful — operate and intermingle with one another.

> The world is not just a physical space traversed by jet planes and full of people running in all directions. It is a complex of responsibilities and options, made out of the loves, the hates, the fears,

the joys, the hopes, the greed, the cruelty, the kindness, the faith, the trust, the suspicion of all.

And we have to see ourselves as part of that complex. For as Merton says, if war comes because nobody trusts anybody, this is because, in part at least, I myself am defensive, suspicious, and untrusting.

If I allow contemplation to set my sights and create my vision, I will know that there are better possibilities. I will believe that we can create a human unity that will recognize our solidarity and communion with one another, or rather that we can recover the unity and solidarity and communion that have always been there, but at a depth that we seem so seldom to reach.

When contemplative prayer or the prayer of awareness becomes not just something I *do* once in a while or even regularly, but rather something that I *am* at all times, then of necessity it moves me to action. Some people think that contemplation calls people into deeper and deeper solitude, and oftentimes it does; but many times it does quite the opposite: it calls me out of solitude to be at the service of my sisters and brothers. For if contemplation gives me the happiness of being at one with all things in that Hidden Ground of Love for which there are no explanations, it will also impel me to do all I can to uncover that "at-oneness," to enable it to be seen. The only way I can do this is by hacking away at all the illusions that keep people apart and perpetuate the fantasy of dualism and spiritual apartheid.

Remember that when Jesus died, the veil in the Temple was torn in two. That veil had been placed there to divide the Holy of Holies (God's part of the Temple) from the Holy Place (the human part of the Temple). We have to remove the veils that seem to separate God from creation and the creation from God. But that is not all. The Holy Place was separated from the court of the people. We need also to remove all the illusory veils that divide us from one another so that we can be aware of our "being at one" with one another. We have to save our world from spiritual apartheid.

We need to work together to create a world where people do not climb over one another to get ahead. A world in which there is no manipulating of people. A world in which poverty and cruelty and terrorism and conflict and war become dimming memories of an abandoned past, not experienced realities of the present. A world where authorities in state and Church function in such a way as to serve the needs of people rather than oppress them and make their lot more difficult.

A Caring World   *What I am really saying is that we have to create a world in which people genuinely care for one another.* And the way to begin this is to start with ourselves: namely, genuinely to care for all those whose lives we touch and even more — those whose lives we could touch if we made the effort to do so. We talk a great deal about the importance in our prayer, in our liturgy, in our ordinary speech of the need for inclusive language. And this concern is of very great importance. For it is not just a matter of language. It is a matter of the way we treat people. Just as we must take seriously the need for inclusive language, so we have to take seriously the responsibility of inclusive care. This is to say that we must not pick and choose those to whom we offer our care. We must care for those whom God has placed in our lives — insofar as we have the time and the resources to do so.

What all this means in detail I am not able to spell out. But we need to have a vision before we can realize it. We need to have a dream before we can bring it to fulfillment. Three attitudes on our part are called for, so it seems to me, if we are to be *genuinely caring persons*: first, a willingness to enter into *dialogue* with people with whom we don't always agree; second, a deep sense of *compassion* (which means the ability to enter into the sufferings of others) and, third, a deliberate, chosen stance of *nonviolence* in all our relationships. These are the attitudes that will enable us to "walk in the Presence of the Lord in the land of the living." These are the ways we must deal with the people we meet "in the land of the living."

Perhaps we can conclude this chapter by reflecting on these three attitudes. *Dialogue* has to do primarily with things of the mind, especially where we have differences with people about how we should think and act. *Compassion* is primarily a matter of the heart that goes out to those in need regardless of how we may disagree with them and their way of thinking. *Nonviolence* is a spirit that characterizes our love for others. What it especially does to our love is to make it unconditional.

Dialogue

Dialogue has as its goal a sharing of the truth. It is not just that I want to share my truth with another. It is also that I want to share the truth the other has that I do not have. A dialogue differs from a debate. The word "debate" comes from Old French and means literally "to batter someone down." "Debate" is a verbal exchange in which you try to win, to get the better of your opponent. But the other is seen as an opponent, an adversary, whom you must "batter down," not physically, but with words.

The etymological derivation of dialogue is quite different. It comes from the Greek verb *legein*, which means "to speak," and the preposition *dia*, which means "across." So "dialogue" means literally "to speak across." You speak "across" the "space" (i.e., the differences) that divides you in order that, by sharing what each of you has to give to the other, you can reduce that space between you. There are two people I know who especially love to talk. When they get together, they vie with one another for the floor. You may know people like that. What they are engaged in is almost simultaneous monologue. They suffer through what the other says, so that they may have their own say. But they don't really *listen*.

Listening, truly listening, really hearing what the other has to say is essential for true dialogue. This isn't always easy. Often we are entrenched in our own position, our own space as it were. It can be threatening at times to listen and find that what others have to say oftentimes makes so much more sense when they say it than when I recall what has been my version of their position. Dialogue can mean a kind of yielding of space, an opening up of what had seemed to be closed frontiers. True dialogue can be an enriching and rewarding experience.

Compassion

Then there is compassion, the movement of the heart striving to share the pain of another. One of the singularly beautiful stories in the Gospels is Jesus' bringing back to life the son of the widow of Naim. It's a picture of pathos, as the funeral procession moves out of the city toward the burial ground. The pathos is heightened when we are told that the woman was a widow (had no husband to support her) and that the son who had died was her only son — which meant that in a very highly patriarchal world she had no support. She was defenseless and alone in a harsh world. And the love of her life was gone.

This story differs from some of the other miracle stories, where Jesus responds to a request that he use his power with God. In this story, the woman simply weeps. She asks for nothing. The only motive for Jesus' mighty action was his *compassion* for her. Not that compassion was not present in the other stories. But here it seems to be the sole motive for Jesus' action.

The word Luke uses for compassion is a curious Greek word, *splanchna*. Literally, it means "entrails," "inner parts." In secular Greek it is used to indicate the inward organs of a person as the seat of their feelings and emotions. We are inclined to be more delicate and refer to the heart as the inner organ that symbolizes a person's deepest feelings. The Greeks were more earthy. "Bowels" was their symbol for a person's most deep-seated emotions. In the Bible the word *splanchna* is invariably used to designate the pity, the mercy, the compassion of God. Some of you may remember older translations of the Bible that spoke of the "bowels of the mercy of God."

By using this rather unusual word for compassion — one generally used only of God — Luke wants us to see in the compassion of Jesus an image of the compassion of God. In his compassion Jesus was most like God. God was acting uniquely in him. But we too are like God when we show compassion. Remember Portia's wonderful courtroom speech on "mercy" in the *Merchant of Venice*, wherein she says that mercy makes us most like God. And this is a good Scriptural perspective. Recall the conclusion of Matthew's Sermon on the Mount: "Be perfect as your Father in heaven is perfect." Luke makes this command seem more possible when he renders it: "Be compassionate as your Father is compassionate."

"The bowels of mercy" may indeed sound earthy, but it makes very graphic the fact that true compassion rises out of the center of our being: where we are most fully ourselves and most profoundly aware of our oneness with God and with our sisters and brothers. The Gospel picture of Jesus' compassion calls us to get inside ourselves and draw forth the marvelous reservoirs of mercy and compassion that are there. Jesus met the widowed mother at the town gate. She was about to cross the threshold of the town where she had lived in peace with her son and enter into the place of death and sorrow. So often we are in a position to touch peoples' lives when they are on that threshold between peace and deep sorrow. We need to be ready to touch them with the bowels of mercy: to be compassionate as Jesus was, as our Father in heaven is compassionate. This surely is "to walk in the Presence of the Lord in the land of the living."

Nonviolence

We have been talking about the attitudes we must bring with us, if we are to walk in God's Presence in the land of the living. I have mentioned dialogue and compassion. I want now to reflect briefly on the third attitude I mentioned: nonviolence. In a sense, nonviolence includes the other two. It presupposes an effort at dialogue. It demands compassion. The term is in some ways unfortunate, because it seems to be negative: not being violent, not hurting anyone. Actually, the other side of nonviolence — that which alone makes it a possible human option — is something very positive, namely, unconditional love.

Nonviolence is not just an attitude toward war, though of course it is that. But the nonviolent position that war is wrong is just one on a whole trajectory of positions that are concerned with the total way in which we live our lives. It's about the way we deal with people, especially when there is disagreement or conflict.

Nonviolence has become very important to me. And when this happens, a kind of revolution takes place in your life. I have come to see so many situations in my life, in dealing with people, where it is so easy to be violent — almost without even intending it. You are caught in violence's webs before you know it. The need to justify ourselves, to prove that we are right and the other person is wrong — these are very human weaknesses that easily lead to violence. And I don't mean violence that hurts people in vicious ways, but in thoughtless ways, in ways that bring out the worst in them instead of the best. I recall a conversation I had on the telephone with a woman who became really violent and ended up slamming down the phone on me. It was only after I had hung up that I realized *I* too had been violent and maybe occasioned her violence. I didn't really say anything particularly violent to her, but I hadn't helped to bring out the good, the truth, in her either. And if I had spoken differently I could have. I have come to see nonviolence relating to so many areas of my

life that would never have occurred to me in the not too distant
past.

Yet nonviolence is not passivity. It has to confront the other
with the truth. But how to do this in a nonviolent way and without giving the smug impression that I have all the truth — this is
the problem and the challenge that nonviolence offers. Also there
is the problem and the challenge to see the truth that is in the
other, the truth that the other is trying to say, but may be saying so poorly that I can never hear it unless I am truly practiced
in nonviolence. There is so much needless misunderstanding between good people, and I am convinced that so often it is because
of hidden aggressions in ourselves that we don't even recognize.

And of course the other side of nonviolence is unconditional
love. It is so easy to withhold love till we believe that the other
is somehow deserving of it. Yet if God reserved divine love till
we really deserved it, where in the world would we be? But God
never holds back love. For God is supremely *contemplative*, which
means that God is immediately and totally aware of everything
in its least detail and utter concreteness. And precisely because
God is contemplative, God is completely *nonviolent*: it would conflict with God's very being to do violence to the things God has
created. God lets things be who they are and what they are. Contemplation and nonviolent love, therefore, are glimpses into the
ineffable: the mystery of God.

Ultimately our nonviolence, like God's, must flow from the
depths of our contemplative life. Our deep awareness that we are
truly "at one with everything and with everyone" in the Hidden
Ground of Love we call God demands of us that we live a nonviolent love. No matter where we are in the world, we "walk in
the Presence of the Lord in the land of the living."

Our responsibility to live nonviolent love, which we can infer
from our reflection on the mystery of God, is made most explicit in the teachings of Jesus that have come down to us from
the early Church. Yet it must be said that the centrality of Jesus'
teaching on nonviolent love has not always been recognized. The
reason for this is that quite a number of teachings of Jesus have
been handed down in the life of the Church and, in dealing with
them, we have not always managed to keep our priorities straight.
Some ages have done better than others. There have been times in
the Church's history (and we have but a few decades ago passed

through such a time), when all the things we believed and practiced seemed to be given equal emphasis. There have been other times when the controversies of a particular age have pushed the church community into the position of emphasizing a particular teaching — sometimes at the expense of others that may actually have been more important.

The Second Vatican Council took note of this recurring problem of preserving a proper balance in what we believe and practice and offered a helpful principle. It says in the document on ecumenism that "when comparing doctrines, [we] must remember that in Catholic teaching there exists an order or hierarchy of truths, since they vary in their relation to the foundation of the Christian Faith." Keeping in mind such a basic principle — that not everything we believe is of equal importance or deserving of equal concern — can be very helpful in determining where we put our energies and emphases in issues that involve faith and morality. The chief problem I have with the radical right in the Roman Catholic Church is that they appear to want to give the same importance to a Vatican prohibition against altar girls as to belief in the Incarnation. Whatever one may think about that particular Vatican prohibition, it would surely be very low in the hierarchy of truths of which the council spoke; for it is hard to see how it could have any possible relationship to the foundation of Christian faith.

But I think that there can be no doubt where the words of Jesus in John 15:12 ("This is my commandment: love one another, as I have loved you") stand in that hierarchy of truths. They are at its very heart and deserve the topmost priority. This love-command of Jesus, which subsumes into itself the values inherent in all other commandments, is a new reality that is Jesus' gift to us. It is not simply a repetition of the general command to love God and neighbor. That was in place long before Jesus came among us. What makes it a new reality and uniquely *his* command is that we are to love, *as he loves us*. In loving we must, so to speak, become him. We must love with his kind of love.

And what was his love? It was an unconditional love. Unconditional *in its intensity*: he was willing to go wherever love would take him, whether to a meal with sinners or to a cross on a hill. It was unconditional *in its extension*: an inclusive love that embraced all women and men, not only his own, his friends, but also the outsiders, the aliens, the marginalized, even those who were his enemies. It was unconditional, too, *in its universal applicability*: it burst the bounds of all legal systems and gave to all commands and laws whatever inner meaning they possess. Finally, it was unconditional *in its motivation*: it rejected any means of encountering another that was not inspired and sustained by love. This means that it repudiated violence and any manipulation of another person; and it had the deepest respect for the truth that is in each and every person.

What I am talking about touches the very nerve-center of Christian faith and it is to be located at that place identified by the Second Vatican Council: namely, the very foundation of Christian faith. We can talk about all manner of things ecclesial and theological. But the root question must always be: do we love one another as Jesus loved us? Are we striving (earnestly, however unsuccessfully) to live what he did: unconditional love? If we are not, then all the discussions we may have about doctrines, beliefs, any other topic whatever, are just so much straw and dust. Indeed, they may well be *evasions*: that is, efforts on our part to do Christian things without having to do the one thing that is essentially Christian — which is to love one another and to do so with no strings attached.

The Johannine writings (the fourth Gospel and John's Epistles) make the utter centrality of love so sparklingly clear. The First Epistle of John simply puts it this way: "One who is without love knows nothing about God" (1 John 4:8). Such people may be able to talk about God or write about God; yet, for all their grand words about God, those without love will simply not know what they are talking about.

For a true Christian loving is like breathing. You can't be alive spiritually without it. To be a living person, you have to be able to breathe. To be an authentic Christian person, you have to be a loving person. Love is at the very center of our lives. When we begin to live (or try to live) from this center, we shall be able to bring love all the way out to the very circumference of that circle that is human life and indeed to all the areas in between, as we "walk in the Presence of the Lord in the land of the living."

I said earlier that "we need to have a dream before we can bring it to fulfillment." The world condition in which we live (though it shows signs of improving) does not always encourage us to hopeful dreams: dreams of a world in which dialogue, compassion, and nonviolence are the highest priorities. Yet, because we believe in the victory of the Resurrection, it is our call as Christians to live in a world of suffering, poverty, terrorism, and the continual threat of a war of mutual massive destruction — and still *dare to hope*.

What does it mean to "dare to hope"? Perhaps one of the important things it means is cleansing our imaginations. To be able to hope for something better, we have to be able to imagine it. Our imagination has been crippled by so much evil that we have almost lost the capacity of imagining what it would be like to live in peace and harmony, in a world where life is not threatened, where air and water are not polluted and where people are genuinely concerned for the true welfare of their sisters and brothers. Such a state of affairs seems like "utopia," the literal meaning of which is "nowhere."

In an issue of *Sojourners*, a journal that has been so passionately dedicated to peace and harmony in the world, there appeared, several years ago, a poem by the fine American poet Denise Levertov. She suggests that it is especially the poet's task to help us cleanse our imaginations: so that we may think true peace and not just the cessation of war. In fact, she tells us that for her writing a poem is like working to achieve peace. She hears a plaintive voice:

> A voice from the dark called out,
> "The poet must give us
> imagination of peace, to oust the intense, familiar
> *imagination of disaster*. Peace not only
> the absence of war."

Then she responds to the voice:

> But peace, like a poem,
> is not there ahead of itself,
> can't be imagined before it is made,
> can't be known except
> in the words of its making,
> grammar of justice,
> syntax of mutual aid.

She tells us we have to learn to think peace, to feel it as a poet begins to feel the rhythm of a poem:

> A feeling toward it,
> dimly sensing a rhythm, is all we have
> until we begin to utter its metaphors,
> learning them as we speak.

We learn about peace (and the harmony and well-being which it embodies), she wants to tell us, only by living it:

> A line of peace might appear
> if we restructured the sentence our lives are making,
> revoking its reaffirmations of profit and power,
> questioning our needs, allowed
> long pauses...
>
> A cadence of peace might balance its weight
> on that different fulcrum; peace, a presence,
> an energy field more intense than war,
> might pulse then,
> stanza by stanza in to the world,
> each act of living
> one of its words, each word
> a vibration of light — facets
> of the forming crystal.

The cleansing of our imagination, the writing of a peace poem, whose words and stanzas are lived and living experiences, are ways of building a truly caring world, in which there will be genuine communication, true compassion, and unconditional love. We work toward such a world, as we "walk in the Presence of the Lord in the land of the living."

5

Obstacles to Awareness

"The Kingdom of heaven is like treasure lying buried in a field."
(Matthew 13:44)

I have spoken about awareness of the Presence of God — that we are in God, that we are one with God — as the fundamental meaning of the experience of prayer. To have this awareness is to experience our unity with God and with the rest of reality. But there is a problem we must face: we cannot have this awareness, this experience of unity with all that is, unless we attain to a deeper level of consciousness than we normally tend to live at.

In this chapter I want to make the point that, if we are to dispose ourselves for that deep awareness of God that is the heart of any true spirituality, we need to look at the kind of awareness we bring to the ordinary life-situation in which we live. One of the problems about our prayer that we have to face concerns not so much what we do at the time we are praying, but what we are doing the rest of the time of our day. So often our awareness of who we are, where we are, what we are doing, and why we are doing it is at a kind of semiconscious level. As Thomas Merton has said: we have the instruments for exploring all sorts of things, but "we can no longer see directly what is right in front of us."

Because we have only a partial awareness of the reality that is right before us, our being is fragmented and divided. This fragmentation and dividedness make it difficult for us to pull ourselves together at the time of prayer. Instead of being recollected (that is, having all the elements of our being gathered into one), we are *distracted* (which is to say, that our energies are scattered in so many directions that we have lost any sense of oneness). If we do not experience a fundamental oneness in ourselves, we can hardly expect that we shall be able to experience our oneness with God. The truth is that so often we lack the ordinary awareness of our own being and of the reality that we experience around us. And it is this ordinary awareness of life that can dispose us for the deep awareness of God's Presence.

I have a very lasting remembrance of one of my seminary Scripture professors. But, curiously, what I remember him for is not what I learned about Scripture, but a quotation that he often confronted us with from *The Imitation of Christ*. The quotation — just three words: *Age quod agis* — was a plea for at least ordinary awareness of what was going on in the class, a class in which, alas, all too many people were doing other things besides studying Scripture. For those who no longer know or remember Latin, *Age quod agis* means "Do what you're doing." "Do the thing that you are supposed to be doing here and now, not something else."

Age quod agis is an important principle of the spiritual life. We need to be doing what we are doing. Someone might want to object: "But isn't that a kind of truism? Aren't we always doing whatever it is we are doing?" The answer is No. Unfortunately in all too many cases, when we are doing something, we are not doing what we are doing. We *seem* to be doing what we are doing, but in reality it may well be that we are doing something else. Perhaps an example will help.

A few weeks ago a young woman came to me whom I had taught in college some years earlier. She had taken a position in social work and had done a fine job of it. After seven or eight years she found, however, that the job had become very stressful. She had a sense of being burnt out and needing to do something else. So I asked her what she might be interested in doing. "Well," she said, "I think I would really like to teach in college. But in order to do so, I would have to get a doctorate and I can't see giving up four years of my life to get ready to do that."

I said to her: "Mary Jane, you need to learn how to wash dishes." "What do you mean?" she asked. "I've done a lot of dish washing. I certainly know how to wash dishes. And what does that have to do with going to university?" I said to her: "Well, maybe you really don't know how to wash dishes. Let me tell you a story." I proceeded to tell her a brief story from a book by Thich Nhat Hanh. Nhat Hanh is a Vietnamese Buddhist monk who opposed the war in Vietnam and who now lives in exile in southern France. The book of his I was referring to is called *The Miracle of Mindfulness*. In it he tells how one day Jim Forest, a leader in the International Fellowship of Reconciliation, was visiting him. They had dinner together. Nhat Hanh's custom was to wash the dishes before serving tea and dessert.

So they finished dinner and Nhat Hanh said he would wash the dishes before getting the tea. Jim offered to do the dishes, while Nhat Hanh was preparing the tea; but Nhat Hanh said, "I am not sure you know how to wash dishes." Jim laughed at him and said, "Of course, I know how to wash dishes. I've been doing it all my life." "No," the monk said, "you would be washing the dishes in order to have your tea and dessert. That is not the way to wash dishes. You must wash dishes to wash dishes."

I believe there is a profounder wisdom in that simple statement than we might at first realize: "You must wash dishes to wash dishes." It's the *Age quod agis* of *The Imitation of Christ*. We must do what we are doing and give our whole attention to it. This is really what "ordinary awareness" is all about: it means doing one thing at a time with full attention, watchfulness, and consciousness. This is the point I was trying to make with my friend, Mary Jane. If she decides to go back to school to get her doctorate, she must not see these years of going to school simply as a means of getting the teaching job she wants to get. She needs to go to school to go to school: to have the enriching experience that such an undertaking could mean. If she goes simply to get a job in the future, she will miss much of what the experience of those years of university life could mean to her. It was important that she be aware of what she was doing each day in her university classes.

I think we all have the tendency to live with only one foot in the present and the other in the past or the future. When this happens, we miss the richness of the present, because we are not really fully aware of it. We aren't fully aware, because we are not fully in the present. So often we do something in order to be able to do something else: our thoughts are so concentrated on that *something else* that we don't really experience what we are doing. We are continually jockeying back and forth between past and future so that we often are *not really there* to the present. We are not truly aware of what is *now*. We don't enjoy what we are doing now, because our thoughts are on what we are going to be doing next. And because our thoughts are diverted away from the present, we are never fully aware of what we are doing here and now.

The Zen master once said to his pupil: "When you walk, walk. When you eat, eat." The pupil said: "But doesn't everyone do this?" "No," the master said, "many people, when they walk are only intent on the place to which they are going. They are not really experiencing the walking. They do not even notice that they are walking. And many people, when they eat, are more involved in making plans about what they will be doing after they eat. This inattention to what they are doing means that they scarcely advert to what they are eating or to the fact that they are eating. They certainly are not taking joy in the awareness of the fact that they are eating."

This kind of absence from the present moment makes it difficult for us to be truly aware. For the *past* is the reality that was, but is no more; the *future* is the reality that will be but is not yet. It is the *present* that is real. If we are out of touch with the present, we are really out of touch with the truly real. This makes it almost impossible for us to shift our attention when we go to pray and have that simple awareness that will enable us to be in touch with God.

All this is to say that attentiveness to the present moment can be a great help toward deepening our awareness of the Presence of God. For such attentiveness to the present moment gathers our being into one. This makes it possible for us more easily to experience our oneness with God.

Why is it so difficult for us to live the present moment, with a vivid attentiveness to what is here and now? Why is it that we seem to be drawn so often away from the present either to the past or to the future? I am sure many factors are involved. I should like to mention two sets of factors: (1) certain things that are a part of our culture and (2) certain things that are a part of our personality structure. Three things in our culture I would like to single out as deterrents to true awareness. They are: (1) our busyness, (2) the addiction of our culture to productivity and efficiency, and (3) quite simply, the noise that saturates our lives so pervasively that we don't seem to be able to escape it.

Obstacles in Our Culture

Let's consider our busyness as a deterrent to awareness and therefore to prayer. So often our energies are being pulled in so many
directions, as diverse responsibilities clamor insistently for our
attention. Writing in 1965 Harvey Cox suggested that the huge
high-rise apartment building and the cloverleafs of our express
highways were the symbols of the 1960s and the new freedoms
that people found to make their friendships wherever they would.
I would venture to say that *the appointment book is the symbol of
our age*. So many of us are slaves to our schedules, keeping this
or that appointment, with one eye on the clock lest we miss the
next one. While we are doing one thing, half our attention is on
what we will be doing next. We act so often as if we belonged
to time and had a responsibility to it instead of time belonging
to us. We have to learn the lesson that there is no way of being
aware "in a hurry." There is no way of seeing what is in front
of us if we are always looking past it. You can't build friendships
on the run. You can't see a flower unless you look at it. Remember what the philosopher Wittgenstein said: "Don't think; look!"
The American poet Georgia O'Keeffe has written poignantly:

> Still — in a way — nobody sees a flower — really — it is so
> small — we haven't time — and to see takes time, like to have
> a friend takes time. (Katherine Hoffman, *An Enduring Spirit: The
> Art of Georgia O'Keeffe*, Scarecrow Press, 1984)

To see takes time. Friendship takes time. Arriving at a sense of
well-being takes time. So too prayer takes time. To hasten through
prayer is hardly to pray.

Roman Catholics need to be especially on the watch for such
"speed-praying." It may be that we acquired this habit because
for so long our liturgy was in a dead language that most of us
did not understand. So why not get it over with as soon as was
decently possible? I remember conducting a retreat at an Anglican
retreat house, the Royal Foundation of Saint Katherine, in the east
side of London. The retreatants were a mixture of Anglicans and
Roman Catholics. After the first session, I invited everyone to say
the Lord's Prayer. It was prayed considerably more slowly than
I was accustomed to hear from Roman Catholic congregations.
The retreatants were surprised when I confidently asserted that

there were more Anglicans among them than Roman Catholics. And my assertion proved correct.

But there is another serious problem that deters us from a true awareness of what *is*, and that is the production-oriented culture we live in and the relentless influence it exercises on us, sweeping us into its feverish compulsion always to be doing things that are useful. Such an attitude is almost fatal to prayer, especially prayer of awareness. For this kind of prayer is not intended to produce anything. Its whole meaning is simply to make us more fully aware of God and of all reality, in other words to make us aware not of something new, but simply aware of what is. To a production-eager society, prayer, since it doesn't produce anything, is probably the most useless thing you could do. To quote Thomas Merton again:

> We are so obsessed with *doing* that we have no time and no imagination left for being.
>
> As a result [people] are valued not for what they are but for what they *do* or what they *have* — for their usefulness. When a [person] is reduced to his function, he is placed in a servile, alienated condition. He exists *for* someone else or even worse for some *thing* else.... Even the fun we have is for a purpose. It is justified not by its gratuity, its simple celebration, but by its utility. It makes us feel better, therefore helps us to function better...get ahead in life.

Why, then, Merton asks, aren't we happy? His answer:

> Because of our servility. The whole celebration is empty because it is "useful." *We have not yet rediscovered the primary usefulness of the useless*. From this loss of any sense of being, all capacity to live for the sake of living,...comes the awful frustrated restlessness of our world obsessed with "doing" so that even "having fun" becomes a job,...a veritable production, even a systematic campaign. (*Conjectures of a Guilty Bystander*, pp. 308–9)

And then finally there is the problem of noise: the noise of planes in the skies, of cars and trucks on our expressways, the radios and the TVs and the machines of all sorts that so fill our lives, more with dissonance than harmony. In our culture's scheme of values there seems to be no room for the luxury of just being alone, for just being silent, for just doing nothing.

If we are really serious about disposing ourselves to live a more contemplative life, we must — to some degree at least — go counterculture. We have to learn to let go of some of the things that clutter our lives so mercilessly. We have to strive to be less busy and more quiet. We have to find a quiet time each day and perhaps also a quiet day at least once a month. God tells us through the psalmist: "Be still and know that I am God." God is One whom we experience in our present. If we want to learn to be aware of God's Presence, we have to learn also to be more fully aware of the present moment.

Obstacles in Our Personality Structure

I mentioned some factors in our culture that tend to blur our awareness of the present: our busyness, our need to produce, the many noises that deafen our inner hearing. I suggested also that there might be factors in our personality structure that may be deterrents to our awareness of the present. One of these personality factors I would like to talk about briefly is our thoughts. Some of you might think that I was offering you a trip back to pre-Vatican II days if I were to say that one of the chief obstacles to our sense of awareness and hence an obstacle to true prayer is quite simply "bad thoughts."

Let me make clear what I mean. Anyone who was a confessor in pre-Vatican II days will remember the frequency with which the mention of "bad thoughts" made their appearance in the confessional. "Bad thoughts" constituted the obsession of many penitents. They took it for granted that every time they went to confession they ought to confess "bad thoughts," for they were sure that such thoughts were ordinary experiences in their lives. They hardly imagined that they could go through a day or at least several days without "having some." That is why it was not uncommon for someone to say: "My last confession was two weeks ago. I had fourteen bad thoughts." They really didn't know how many such thoughts they had experienced, but they felt they were probably on the safe side if they figured on about one a day. Others would go beyond the bounds of all probability and, just to make sure they did not minimize this very bad habit, would confess: "My last confession was two weeks ago. I had fourteen hundred bad thoughts." As a confessor hearing such an admission, one had to wonder if this person actually had time to do anything else during the week except to have "bad thoughts." It seemed like it would take a good deal of time to have fourteen hundred thoughts, whether good or bad.

Mercifully that period of the Church's existence has pretty much disappeared — and for good. People no longer prepare for the sacrament of reconciliation by trying to figure out: "how many bad thoughts did I have since my last confession?" They are concerned to question themselves about much more important lapses in fidelity to the Gospel.

Yet, all this being happily so, I still want to suggest that one of our serious problems in striving to pray well, in striving to be aware of God, is "bad thoughts." Let me clarify what I mean when I say that discovering how to deal with "bad thoughts" is one of the very important steps toward praying better.

First of all, when I speak of "bad thoughts," I am not thinking of the kind of thoughts that so many young men used to confess, namely, the thoughts they experienced when they saw a pretty woman with an attractive body and took genuine pleasure in seeing her. To describe such a thought as "bad" simply shows how strong had been our attachment to the Gnostic heresy (that considered matter evil), in spite of the fact that Gnosticism had been condemned by the Church centuries ago.

When I speak of "bad thoughts," I have something quite different in mind. Or, if one wants to include certain kinds of sexual thoughts in the category of "bad thoughts," I would tend to put them very low on the list of thoughts that wreak havoc with our effort to pray, our desire to be aware of God. When I speak of "bad thoughts," I am thinking of the kinds of thoughts that divide us, that fragment our being, that undo our inner unity. I am thinking of the thoughts that keep us chained to the past or that thrust us out of the present into the future. What I have in mind are, for instance, thoughts of anger: not just the momentary anger that a particular situation may give rise to, but the anger that is harbored and nursed, the anger that wants to show up another, get even with him or her, prove yourself right and them wrong. I have in mind thoughts of dissatisfaction with my life-situation. Again I don't mean a momentary thing, but something that is dwelled on, something I hold others responsible for and continue to sulk, interiorly, because no one seems concerned to change the things that I think ought to be changed. I have in mind thoughts of selfishness and self-seeking and wounded pride. Thoughts of jealousy and distrust, the desire to "get even" with someone who I believe has mistreated me. Thoughts of animosity and violence. Thoughts of resentment, bitterness, and hurt feelings that can be an especially damaging temptation to people who don't always have a strong "support system."

These brooding, disturbing thoughts in us represent what is really a false, illusory self in us, a self that is untrue to our best instincts, a self that is untrue to the image of God that we are. It is this false and illusory self that can prevent me from being my true self, able to live in full awareness of the present moment and therefore properly disposed to that awareness of the Presence of God — which is the heart of prayer.

Another factor that can be part of our personality structure, at least at times, is the good old-fashioned fault of "sloth." Those who recall the catechism will remember it as something especially bad, since it was one of the "capital" (source) sins, or even more sinister (though not really correct), one of the "deadly" sins. The English word "sloth" tends to designate the quality of being terribly slow, always being tardy, never getting things done. It was a fault taken very seriously by the medieval theologians and, before them, by the monks of the Egyptian desert. They called it *acedia* and wrote all sorts of treatises about it. They saw it a bit differently from the way we think of it. For them it was something that affected the heart as the center of human consciousness. Etymologically, it has an interesting origin, deriving from the Greek word *kedos*, which means "care." When you add the "a" ("alpha privative") to it, it turns out to mean "not caring." It's a lackluster attitude, an I-don't-give-a-damn frame of mind, a lack of enthusiasm, a joylessness in whatever we do. The monks called *acedia* the noonday demon (*daemon meridianus*): the demon that assaults you not at night, but during the day, during the time we are called upon to carry out our responsibilities to our sisters and brothers. (Perhaps this is the reason the monks always took a siesta after the noonday meal.) It is so easy to let this "demon" accompany us through our daily tasks so that we do them gloomily, cheerlessly, without joy. Worth noting is that St. Thomas Aquinas saw *acedia* as opposed to the "joy of love." He opposes it, not to love, but to the joy that ought to accompany love. *Acedia* is a state of depression, in which, even if we do the loving thing, we experience no happiness in doing it. What we do is done half-heartedly. This means that we cannot really be attuned to the present moment because half of us is not even there.

There is a Zen story about a man who finds himself being stalked by a tiger. He runs only to see that he is on the edge of a cliff. He grabs some vines and lets himself down over the side of the cliff. Looking up he sees the tiger sniffing at him menacingly from above. He looks down and to his dismay — guess what? — there is another tiger at the bottom of the cliff, looking every bit as ferocious as the one above. The man looks at the vines and is somewhat distressed to see two mice gnawing at the vines. Then all at once he sees, tangled in the vines, a beautiful, large strawberry. He reaches for it, plucks the strawberry, and enjoys its luscious taste.

If you happen to find this story a bit much, something of an overstatement of our need to be alert to the reality of the present, you might find it easier to deal with a delightful poem written by R. S. Thomas, a Welsh poet who is an Anglican priest. Called "The Bright Field," this poem sums up what I am trying to say about our deep spiritual need of being aware of the reality of the present moment, of living now.

The poet makes clear to us that every moment, if we saw it aright, could be like Moses' vision — seeing the burning bush: a bush on fire yet not consumed, a bush whose fire betokened the Saving Presence of God. At any moment we can be aware of God, for God is there. Every moment hides the "pearl of great price." Every moment the "treasure" is there in the field for us to unearth. Here are the poet's words:

> I have seen the sun break through
> to illumine a small field
> for a while, and gone my way
> and forgotten it. But that was the pearl
> of great price, the one field that had
> the treasure in it. I realize now
> that I must give all that I have
> to possess it. Life is not hurrying
>
> on to a receding future, nor hankering after
> an imagined past. It is the turning

aside like Moses to the miracle
of the lit bush, to a brightness
that seemed as transitory as your youth
once, but is the eternity that awaits you.

6

Helps to Awareness: Letting Go, Waiting, Accepting

"The meaning is in the waiting."
(R. S. Thomas)

Some years ago I was visiting a friend in Norway. One day we went to one of the outdoor museums for which Norway is famous and there we saw a reconstructed medieval stave church. One of the interesting features of these churches is that around three-quarters of the church was an outdoor porch. It was there not for visiting or social purposes. It was built there so that the men would have a place to put their weapons when they came to church. Before entering the church, they left their guns and slings and bows and arrows outside the church door.

Letting Go

This is not a bad image with which to begin a chapter whose intent is to discuss the atmosphere of life we need to create if we are to foster a true inner life and make prayer of awareness a valued element of that life. Think of the time you give to the prayer of awareness as a brief period in your day when, at least for these few moments, you let fall from your grasp the "slings and arrows of outrageous fortune" and even, if I may put it this way, the slings and arrows of good fortune. This is a time of letting go of the things that encumber us. For we come to prayer, at least this kind of prayer, not to solve our problems, but to set them aside (put brackets around them at least for the time being) — so that by doing nothing and becoming empty, we can restore some measure of unity and depth to our lives.

In a letter to a Benedictine nun, written November 16, 1967, Merton replied to her request for suggestions about what a retreat ought to be. It ought not to be highly organized, he insists. There should be less pressure and "more time simply to get oneself back in one's right mind." One thing he emphasizes is the need of being "empty" and "doing nothing." Point four of the five suggestions he offers for the structuring of a retreat is the following:

> I would suggest that even for those who find silence and solitude oppressive: there is a certain value in just disciplining oneself to be "empty" and to spend a certain time *doing nothing*. Those who can try an hour a day of this will soon find that instead of going nuts they may profit by it more than they expected. Walking in the garden is permitted in such "empty" periods, but no talking, no reading, no formal prayer, just plain nothing. (Unpublished, at the Thomas Merton Studies Center, Louisville, Ky.)

Merton is, of course, speaking of a time of retreat, but what he says can, in properly modified form, be said of daily wordless prayer. We all need to heed this suggestion: we do need to let go, if only for the short period of our prayer, and do nothing. Most of us are not very good at "doing nothing." We may be experts in "wasting time." But "wasting time" is not the same thing as "doing nothing." "Wasting time" is doing *nothing significant*, but doing nothing significant, however understood, is still something we *do*. We find it difficult simply to stop doing; yet we need to let it happen in our lives.

Some of the things we let go of during prayer we may have to pick up again after our prayer. But if our prayer is consistent, we will pick them up with greater strength and inner calm, because in our prayer we will have moved toward a certain degree of personal unity. Once we have found our own center, it is easier to deal with the things that are on the periphery.

The things we have to pick up again and deal with may be duties at work and at home, familial responsibilities and societal ones. These we cannot evade, though at times they may impose heavy burdens on us. We have to learn to recognize God's Presence in these tasks that our life-situation places upon us: God's

Presence in the land of the living. *Letting go* of everything for a brief time each day and *simply being* during that time, will help us to grasp an essential principle of well-being, namely, that, no matter how much there is that we must do, it is not our *doing*, but our *being* that enables us to identify who we are. A life spent in doing can be very destructive of human persons, if they never come to know the personal identity of the one who does all these things. Well-doing by itself can never bring well-being.

The theme of "letting go" reminds me of the two monks who were walking together and came upon a swift-flowing stream. A young woman was standing bewildered at the water's edge: the stream was too swift for her to dare wading across it. Thereupon one of the monks picked her up and carried her across. He let her down. She thanked him and went on her way. The two monks continued their walk. There was silence for some time. Then the other monk said to the one who had carried the young girl across the river: "Why did you pick her up and carry her across the river?" The first monk looked at him and said: "You're still carrying her, aren't you?"

While it is true that there are certain things that we can let go of only momentarily, because they call us to responsibilities that we cannot shirk, there are ever so many things that it would serve our health and well-being to let go of permanently. In many areas of our lives "letting go" needs to be, not just a momentary experience that continues only for the brief time set aside for prayer; it has to become a way of life for us. There is a fair amount of excess baggage we still carry around with us from our past. There are the wounds and the bruises we have experienced in body and spirit, as we have traveled life's journey from childhood onward. Some of these hurts may be such that we need help to be able to let go of them. Others we hang on to, mostly because we enjoy nursing them. It is a kind of psychological greed in us or, if you will, a lack of true poverty. For the opposite of poverty is not wealth, but greed, not possessions, but possessiveness. Possessiveness is the desire to have, to cling to things, to clutch them to ourselves. The most destructive form of possessiveness is not a clinging to material things, but to less clearly definable realities. There can be a possessiveness that refuses to let go of our prejudices and biases. A possessiveness that clings to my time and my convenience and is unwilling to let go of these when others may need me. There can be a clinging to old, familiar, trodden paths, when God and the needs of the Christian community may be calling us to venture into the realm of the new, the untried, the unfamiliar — with only the Gospel to guide us. And there is that final clinging we have to let go of, whether we want to or not: the clinging to life that is prompted by the fear of death.

The three summers before I was ordained to the priesthood I spent as a counselor at Camp Columbus on Owasco Lake, one of New York State's charming finger lakes. When I first became a counselor, I didn't know how to swim. This posed a slight problem, because as a counselor, I also had the responsibility of serving as a lifeguard on the waterfront. Happily no one drowned as a result of my ineptitude; in fact under the tutelage of one of the other counselors, I managed to learn to swim. Take it from me, it is much harder to learn to swim as an adult than as a child. When you learn to swim as an adult, you are more reflective about it. Thinking about all that it demands of you hinders you from achieving the spontaneity that makes swimming easier and more effortless. One of the things you soon come to realize is that, if you ever expect to be able to swim, you must learn to "let go." You have to let go of your rigidity, your stiffness, your fear for your own security. You have to let these go and abandon yourself to the water. Only then will you be able to swim.

We all swim in an ocean of divine love and mercy. But we have to become aware of it. This can only happen when we let go of all that we cling to and abandon ourselves joyfully to that love and mercy. And the last thing we have to let go of is the self that clings. When at last we are able to do this, there is then nothing of us. There is only God and we are in God.

"Letting go" is never easy and we can never be quite sure that we have done it for good. The temptation to take up again what we have let go, to return to our "clinging," can linger as an all too present allurement, especially when we are dealing with strong "attachments" or "addictions." I am reminded of the little boy who was out shopping with his mother. After they had been in the store for some time, the little boy said: "Mommy, I have to go to the bathroom." His mother said to him: "Now you just hold it for a while and we'll hurry home." They were part way home when all at once the little boy had an "accident." His mother, exasperated, said to him: "I told you to hold it till we got home."

His plaintive answer was: "I was doing what you said. But then I 'let go' for a better hold."

One thing should be made very clear: "letting go" is by no means a merely negative experience. It is a wholesome way of overcoming the rigidity of fixed patterns of behavior over which we seem to have little control. It brings a spirit of freedom and spontaneity into our lives. If an airplane is overloaded with excess baggage, it may not be able to get off the ground. Sometimes it may be necessary to get rid of that baggage in order that the plane may be free to fly. We too may have to get rid of excess baggage in order to fly — that is, to lift ourselves up above our superficial selves to find our true selves in God. We have to let go in order to be *aware*.

Thus it may be said that *letting go* is the *ascetical* dimension of the Christian life, while *awareness* is the *contemplative* dimension. The first exists for the second. We must learn to *let go* in order that we may *be aware*. "Letting go" can be a very exhilarating experience: to feel that at last I am free, unencumbered. But, though a good, even wondrous, experience in itself, it is never an end in the Christian life. We want to be free in order that we may be *aware* of ourselves, of God, of all reality. We want to be able to see reality as it is. The love and the peace that are at the center of all that is. The unity of our lives that is experienced at the center of our being or, if you will, in our hearts.

Waiting

We may sometimes have the uncomfortable feeling that the time spent reading about the prayer of awareness may be more enjoyable than the time we give to that prayer. For it is one thing to be told and really to believe through faith that we are in God. It is another thing to experience that Presence. Experiencing the holy Presence is always a gift that we welcome gratefully if and when it comes. But we cannot command it. God remains master of the divine gifts. We may go through long periods of time being faithful to wordless prayer and seeming not to experience much of anything. We cling by faith to our belief that we are in the Presence of God. But to experience that belief, to experience God, this we have to *wait for*. It is important for our spiritual well-being that we realize that the waiting is not just putting in time. The waiting itself has meaning.

In the hurried, frenzied culture in which we live it is difficult to see waiting as anything better than a chore. Waiting taxes our patience. We wait in a traffic line because there is an accident up ahead. We wait in a supermarket because there were so many insensitive people who decided to shop at the same time we did. Children wait to get through grade school so that they can get to high school; then they wait this out so they can get to college. Then they wait for that life of independence that they suppose comes after college. We wait for a friend to come to visit us and are perturbed or anxious because the friend is late. We wait for the flu bug to leave our system so that we can carry on our lives as usual.

So much of life is waiting, and so often the waiting means nothing more than frustration. "Waiting" is something we have to put up with. It has to be endured.

Creative Waiting But there is a another kind of waiting. There is the waiting of a mother for her child to be born and that waiting is the joy of life growing within her. There is the waiting of a writer for an inarticulate idea that has come to her mind to be formed finally into a clear and forceful statement. The waiting for the plot to unfold, as we read an absorbing story. Waiting for a son or daughter or a niece or nephew or the child of a friend to grow up to the maturity that the brightness of youth promises. There is the waiting for the right answer to a question, as I begin to grasp the elements of the question and as my struggling with them moves me in the direction of the answer; but for the fullness of the answer, I shall have to wait.

This type of waiting is not the "waiting of frustration"; on the contrary, it is a waiting of joyous expectation. It is not just time to be put in but time to be enjoyed. Such waiting is to be reveled in. For the joy of expectation participates in the joy of fulfillment. Part of the joy of a trip is planning it. Part of the joy of getting to a destination is the journey that gets you there. This is the kind of waiting that belongs to the liturgical season of Advent. We await the Lord's coming with the realization that he is already in our midst; but since we are not fully aware of his Presence, we have to wait for our own consciousness to catch up with reality. But the waiting is living with the Mystery that is to come. It is watching it unfold. It is readying the atmosphere that makes that unfolding possible. Waiting is sinking into the meaning of the Mystery.

There is a poem by R. S. Thomas, the Anglican priest and Welsh poet whom I have already referred to, that captures this understanding of that waiting which is pregnant with meaning. In the poem entitled "Kneeling," he pictures himself kneeling before an altar just before he is to preach. There is a silence in the air, like a staircase from heaven. Sunlight rings the preacher as he kneels, just before he takes on his role as God's spokesperson. He asks God to prompt him in what he says; yet even though God speaks through him, he realizes only too well — as every preacher must — that something will be lost. People will have to wait. It will take time for God's meaning to sink into their hearts. But the meaning will emerge from the waiting.

> Moments of great calm,
> Kneeling before an altar
> Of wood in a stone church
> In summer, waiting for the God
> To speak; the air a staircase
> For silence; the sun's light
> Ringing me, as though I acted
> A great role. And the audiences
> Still; all that close throng
> Of spirits waiting, as I,
> For the message.
>   Prompt me, God;
> But not yet. When I speak,
> Though it be you who speak
> Through me, something is lost.
> The meaning is in the waiting.
>   (*Selected Poems, 1946–1968*,
>   p. 119)

Accepting

Earlier I voiced a warning against what I labeled "spiritual apartheid," a way of viewing reality that would separate God from creation. This same spiritual affliction can segregate my inner life from my life in the world, as if they were two separate realities.

When this happens, an exclusive priority is given to such a separate inner life and the impression is created that it alone matters.

My task as a Christian and indeed as a human being is to accept reality in its fullness. This means accepting the fact that my spirituality encompasses my total existence, not just a part of it. It means accepting the truth of who I am, but that truth in its concreteness and historicity. Accepting who I am, therefore, includes affirming the "when," the "where," and all the circumstances of that concrete historicity.

Among other things, this involves accepting my contingency, the radical dependence on God that stamps my identity, and the limitations this places on who I am and what I am able to become. While I may be said to possess an almost unlimited potential, still I have only finite capabilities for realizing that potential. I cannot achieve everything I am capable of achieving. Making a particular choice in my life prevents me from choosing other options that are incompatible with that choice. Accepting reality means being ready to live with the choices I have made. This does not mean, of course, that if I make what turns out to be an obviously poor choice, I should not change. At the same time flitting from one choice to another fragments one's existence and makes it difficult to live a unified life.

Gifts   Accepting the reality of my own existence in all its historicity means recognizing and striving, within the obvious limits of that historicity, to actualize the gifts that I have received. Natural endowments and graces of the spirit are blessings of God to be accepted with gratitude, sensitivity, and joy; at the same time they are burdens that impose responsibilities that at times weigh heavily on the human spirit. Gifts are not bank accounts that we can simply draw on at will. They are, to change the metaphor, rough stones that have to be polished, sometimes at the cost of pain and suffering, before their true beauty can come to light. They are seeds sown in our liberty that come to fruition only with struggle; and the greater the gifts — so it seems — the greater will be the struggle to actualize them. There are two ways of seeing one's gifts. We may look upon them as if they belonged to us by our own right; then — because this is illusion — they easily become occasions for pride and self-adulation. But if we realize that they are received and unearned, they can be occasions for true humility (in a very literal sense of putting us in touch with the ground: the Ground of our being). We can use our gifts to promote self-aggrandizement or to help create a better world; or we can be lazy and let them lie fallow and uncultivated. It is by appreciating the gifts of mind and heart, of body and spirit and striving to develop them fully and unselfishly that we are able to achieve a measure of integration and unity in our lives. We build our identity through the ways in which we utilize our gifts of nature and grace; or rather we discover our identity — an identity that exists at the deepest level of our being and that is manifested in our various gifts. The person we are able to become (i.e., the person we are in our depths) is hidden in our gifts.

Accepting my gifts has as a fairly obvious corollary a willingness to accept my own faults and the responsibility I have for them. Till I acknowledge them as mine, I cannot move to eradicate them. Till I consciously own them, I cannot consciously strive to disown them.

Relationships   Accepting the truth of my existence means accepting the relationships that life brings to me and realizing that these relationships are also gifts: gifts that come to me because I live in a particular time and place. I do not exist in isolation, but in a series of interlocking relationships that, like the gifts I possess, play a necessary role in my achieving and discovering who I am as a person. Relationships may be crippling or they may be life-sustaining. They may hinder growth or enhance it. If they are wholesome gifts, they build up community where there is a blossoming of gifts and a nurturing of life. Yet, while it is true that I do not exist in isolation, still I need some element of solitude in my life if my contribution to community is to be anything more than superficial. In the frenetic culture in which we live, solitude is not easy to come by. We have to plan it into our lives if it is not to slip away altogether.

Solitude and Community   Thomas Merton, whose monastic life made it much easier for him to find solitude, yet faced throughout his life the tensions we all encounter in balancing solitude and community. Some time ago I wrote an article "Thomas Merton: The Gregarious Solitary." Describing a "solitary" as one who chooses to be alone and a "gregarious person" as someone who has a strong liking for being with other people, I tried to set up a causal relationship between his solitude and his gregariousness. I wanted to make the point that it was because he sought solitude that he found people. His need for relationships with people, in other words, was not a chink in the armor of his solitude — a regrettable defect that a solitary must strive to overcome. Rather solitude helped him to realize his solidarity with other people: his need for them and his duties toward them. He was not a solitary just for himself; he was a solitary for them too.

One of the tasks we face if the prayer of awareness is to have a directive force in our lives is to find a suitable balance between the relationships that knit us to other people and the solitude we need if we are to nourish the inner aspects of those relationships and in this way contribute to the building of true community.

I find a helpful insight for dealing with such a balance in an entry that Thomas Merton made in his journal under the date of December 29, 1949, which he included in the first draft of what was to become *The Sign of Jonas*, but which for some reason he removed (or — a more sinister thought — had been removed by the censors). In this excised entry he speaks of a "spiritual narcissism" and wonders whether there might be an element of it in his enthusiasm for solitude. Then he writes: "Narcissistic solitude is a substitute for the responsibility of living with people." He then offers a contrast, saying: "At the other pole is the crass activism that delights in company and noise and movement and escapes the responsibility of living at peace with God." Anyone who is intent on living a true inner life must avoid both these extremes: a narcissistic solitude on the one hand and a crass activism on the other. Both — though they move in different directions — are forms of escape from life and reality. Merton then proceeds to make a most significant point for understanding relationships in our lives:

> Our whole life must be a dialectic between community and solitude. Both are tremendously important, and our contemplative life subsists in the fruitful antagonism between these two terms. ("The Whale and the Ivy," 3:22, unpublished)

Tensions   We need solitude in order to discover the things that make for true community. Yet we must be prepared for the fact that people committed to solitude and prayer may not always be in agreement as to what is best for the community — whether that community be the family, the parish, the religious community, the national community, the community of the churches. Thus, for example, what the Church in Latin America has learned from its solitude and reflection may not agree with what Vatican officials have concluded from their own prayerful reflection. Inevitably we are going to take sides on these and other issues in the life of the church community; yet it would be sad if we did not talk with one another and through further solitude and reflection let the Spirit of God who is the Spirit of unity help us to work out the tensions that, given the humanness of all of us who make up the Church, are bound to arise. In the words I quoted from Merton, he spoke of the dialectic that must go on between solitude and community; but he also said that a community that is truly contemplative will be kept alive ("subsist" is his word) in the context of the "fruitful antagonism" that will inevitably mark that dialectic. "Antagonism" is a strong word; yet I am sure we feel it in our own personal dialectic between solitude and community, as well as in the dialectic of the Church. What is important is that the "antagonism" be *fruitful*.

Accepting such antagonism and working to make it fruitful is but another aspect of accepting the truth of who I am in the concreteness and historicity of my own life situation.

Acceptance and Rejection   Not every antagonism is fruitful and not everything that is part of my concrete existence at a particular moment of history is acceptable. Acceptance of the true and the real demands rejection of the false and the illusory. If I am to pray the prayer of awareness, I have to say a strong No to all the injustices that demean human persons, manipulate them, rob them of their dignity, marginalize them in such a way that they are unable to live their lives in decency, calm, and peace. In the preface to the Japanese edition of *The Seven Storey Mountain* (written in August of 1963) Merton expresses the stance of refusal that must accompany all true acceptance. He tells his Eastern readers that his monastery is not a way of "escape" from the world, but the place where, in the context of the life he has adopted — a life that is essentially nonassertive and nonviolent — he takes his part in the struggles and sufferings of the world. Thus he writes:

It is my intention to make my entire life a rejection of, a protest against the crimes and injustices of war and political tyranny which threaten to destroy the whole race of man and the world with him. By my monastic life and vows I am saying NO to all the concentration camps, the aerial bombardments, the staged political trials, the judicial murders, the racial injustices, the economic tyrannies, and the whole socio-economic apparatus which seems geared for nothing but global destruction in spite of all its fair words in favor of peace. I make monastic silence a protest against the lies of politicians, propagandists and agitators...

If I say NO to all these secular forces, I also say YES to all that is good in the world and in human beings. I say YES to all that is beautiful in nature, and in order that this may be a yes of freedom and not of subjection, I must refuse to possess anything in the world purely as my own. I say YES to all the men and women who are my brothers and sisters in the world, but for this yes to be an assent of freedom and not of subjection, I must live so that no one of them may seem to belong to me, and that I may not belong to any of them.

Accepting reality helps me to pray the prayer of awareness. For my prayer means accepting the most important reality of all, the Reality that underlies all else that is real: namely, that I am *in God*, which means that I am *in* Love. God's Love contains me, sustains me, even as that Love has given me my very existence. There can be no greater joy than that which comes to each one of us when we accept the fact that God accepts us.

7

Talking about God

Much has been said thus far about prayer as awareness of God's Presence. The time has come to say something about God in whose Presence we are. Traditionally, those who talk about God are called theologians. That is what "theologian" means: a person who speaks words about God. Since the beginnings of scholasticism (in the twelfth century) we have come to understand the theologian as someone who reflects on data — the data of revelation, Church documents, etc. — and then tries to organize this material into some kind of coherent speech about God and things related to God.

What Is a Theologian?

I need to point out that this was not the way people understood the theologian in the early centuries of the Church (before the rise of scholasticism) nor is it the understanding in the Orthodox Church today. For the early Church the theologian was the *saint*. That is to say, he or she was the person who had experienced God and who wrote about God out of that experience. There were other people in the Church who were also saints (since they too had experienced God), but they did not have the gift of articulating that experience. So the theologians expressed not only their own experience of God, but also the experience of the Holy Presence that was going on in the life of the community of the faithful.

This, I think, is an understanding of theology that it would be helpful for us to return to (it is still the understanding that prevails in the Eastern Christian Churches). Let the theologian become once again the person who articulates the experience of God that goes on in the community of God's people.

The Theologian's Limitations

But whether the theologian works from data in documents or data from experience, he or she would be the first to admit that the articulation never reaches the level of the experience. There is a miracle story narrated in the seventh chapter of Mark's Gospel (31–37) that tells of the cure of a deaf man who is described as having a "speech impediment." The words he "had a speech impediment" are actually a translation of one single word in Greek. It is the Greek word *mogilalos*; and "having a speech impediment" accurately translates the word. It could also be given a one-word translation: "stammerer." The Gospel story can be seen as a picture of all of us. As we stand before the mystery of God revealed in Christ, we are all *mogilaloi*: we are all "stammerers." That might be a good definition of a theologian: "a stammerer in the face of the reality of God." Jesus was able to cure the deaf man of this physical impediment, but it is only the direct vision of God that could possibly cure us of the speech impediment we have in talking about God.

Good theologians understand this. They know that all they say can never even approximate the experience. So much is lost between the experience and the articulation. Theological words and definitions and treatises are like matches lighted by our experiences to help us look at the sun. The fact is that we *can* look at the matches, but we *cannot*, without losing our sight altogether, look at the sun. That means that when we want to talk about God or think about God, we have no other choice: we have to use the matches.

But when we have the experience, when we are fully aware, when we look at the Sun, we not only cease "stammering," because we have nothing to say; we also no longer use the matches. We can't even see them (nor do we have any desire to), for the brightness of the Sun blinds us by its brilliance. We really see because we can't see. We really are silent, for we have no words (and no desire for any). But when the inner eyes of the mind are darkened and I am no longer *thinking about* or trying to *talk about* God, then the inner eyes of the heart are opened and I am able to grasp God (or rather be grasped by God) in the embrace of love. I mentioned in chapter 2 that awareness of God is not so much something we do but something we are. I also said it was not *thinking about God*.

What is it that we *are* when we are aware of God? I would venture to say that our whole contemplative tradition would back me up in asserting that we are contemplatives because we are *lovers of God*. The anonymous work of the fourteenth century that has come into such prominence in recent years, *The Cloud of Unknowing*, speaks for that tradition when it says: "God can be taken and held by love, not by thought."

Experiences of a Theologian

I would suggest, then, that theologians should have two kinds of experiences: (1) the experience of the heart (their own as well as that of the community of faith) that "knows" God through love, and (2) the experience of the mind thinking and reflecting on the experience of the heart and attempting to do the impossible, namely, to express the inexpressible or, to use Alan Watts's words, "to eff the ineffable." No matter how great their writing skills may be, the occupational affliction of all theologians is an inadequacy and an ineptitude in saying "God."

This is not to say that theology is of no value to us. We need to hear these articulations of what goes on in the depths of the human heart. They can help us to understand what may be happening in our own lives. But we need to keep our priorities straight: what is happening is more important than what can be said about it. What is going on in human hearts needs to be expressed, but whatever the expression may be, the experience is what truly matters. The best theologians will be lovers before they speak and, better still, also while they speak. What a great bumper sticker this could make: "Theologians are the best lovers."

I am reminded, as I say this, of a meeting I had a few weeks ago with a young couple. They had asked me to preside at their wedding. The bride was a practicing Catholic and the daughter of dear friends of mine. The young man was a baptized Roman Catholic, twenty-nine years of age, who had at the age of eighteen, so he told me, made the decision that he could no longer accept the theistic position that God exists.

I had a long talk with him before the wedding. He seemed to be a fine person and a quite intelligent young man. I resisted the temptation to say to him: "You have a difficulty in that you have a problem about the existence of God. You would surely have much greater difficulty if God had a problem about your existence." I also refrained from using the nineteenth-century apologetics for proving the existence of God that I had learned so carefully in the seminary and that, for too many years, I taught so self-complacently to unwary college students.

In fact, I suggested to him that he was probably wasting his time talking about proofs for the existence of God and deciding he couldn't accept them. Nobody really comes to faith in God because they have accepted proofs for God's existence. Such proofs may make sense after one has already come to believe, but seldom before. (This, I take it, is the whole point of the "five ways" of St. Thomas Aquinas for "proving" the existence of God. Aquinas was not writing for nonbelievers to convert them to belief. His words were for believers to help them appreciate the reasonableness of the belief they already held.) I said to my young friend: "Even if I could convince you that there is some being outside you whom people call God, your knowledge that God existed would simply be another truth to place alongside other truths you accept. It would be like proving to you that another continent existed, or another planet. The truth about God, if there is any, isn't going to mean anything to you until you are willing to open your heart to the possibility that you can experience that which transcends you and yet somehow is within you. Then you will have not just another truth to hold on to. What you experience will challenge you and make demands on you. And you will find yourself, almost unaccountably, wanting to respond to the challenge and meet the demands."

I offered a parallel for my young friend to consider: his belief in the existence of the love he had for the woman he was about to marry. He was firmly convinced of the reality of that love. Yet I doubt that he would be able to give to anyone, except her, truly convincing proofs of his love for her. And to her he didn't have to prove it, because she had already come to believe in the reality of his love for her. For she had experienced it in their relationship with one another. She had come to know, as he had too, the demands that love makes on a person and the strong desire it gives one to meet those demands.

I said to him: "You will never find God by looking for proofs that God exists. In fact, you will never find God by looking outside yourself. You will only find God within. It will only be when you have come to experience God in your own heart and let God into the corridors of your heart (or rather found God there) that you will be able to 'know' that there is indeed a God and that you are not separate from God."

I have no way of knowing whether anything I said to him made any impression on him or whether I even have any right to expect that it might. I can only hope, for the good of both of them, that he may be able to open his mind and heart to the God who, at least I believe, is there, if he will only look in the right place or, better, in the right way.

One of the things that this dialogue brought home to me was the realization of how necessary and yet how difficult it is for us to *speak* about God. We think of God. We pray to God. We adore God. We try to be aware of God's Presence. But when we try to talk about God, we are all "stammerers." We are tongue-tied: we simply don't have adequate words to speak about God. However deeply we may experience God, God always remains Mystery and we can never articulate the Mystery with a clarity that is at all adequate. We are, as I suggested, like the deaf man in the Gospel, who had a speech impediment.

It is helpful to read through all the Gospels and see that even those who had the immediate experience of God present in Jesus were "stammerers" when they came to talk about that experience. Think of the scene midway into each of the Synoptic Gospels: the profession of faith of Peter. Mark's narrative is probably the closest to what actually happened. He has Peter say: "You are the Messiah." This was a great leap of faith, surely, for them to make. It went far beyond what the others had to say about Jesus. Yet there was so much growth that still had to happen: the Easter faith expressed by the disciples goes far beyond Peter's profession at Caesarea Philippi. Compared to Thomas's "my Lord and my God," Peter's words at Caesarea Philippi amount to mere "stammering." And even those wondrous words of Easter, when we compare them with the divine reality, still remain little more than "stammering."

The Root Problem

At the root of the problem posed by theological language is the fact that all the knowledge we have of God comes from some human experience of God. The words we possess are able to express only the human experience, not the divine reality experienced. It is for this reason that all our language about God is symbolic, metaphorical. When we speak of God we are always using analogies.

Analogy

It will be worth our while, therefore, to devote a bit of time to clarifying the meaning of analogy. If anyone is eager for a general definition of analogy, here is one from *The Concise Oxford Dictionary of the Christian Church* (edited by E. A. Livingston, 1977):

> A method of predication whereby concepts derived from a familiar object are made applicable to a relatively unknown object in virtue of some similarity between two otherwise dissimilar objects. Thus it is "by analogy" that it is possible for the human intellect to speak of the justice of God, for, though God's justice is not totally unlike justice encountered in human experience, it is not identical with it.

I doubt that this definition has sent quivers of excitement through your entire nervous system. Nor, I suspect, will your heart start palpitating with unseemly rapidity when I point out that the attribute that you predicate of the two objects (or subjects) is called the "analogon" and that the two objects (or subjects) are called the "analogates." Thus in the example given in the definition above, "justice" would be the "analogon"; God and people in whom we experience what we call "justice" would be the "analogates." If we were to give a personality to the *analogon*, we might conceive it as a Janus-like figure with two faces, each looking in opposite directions. Each of the faces would want to make a speech. The one (the "Yes" face) would say: "The analogates are similar," while the other (the "No" face) would say with equal conviction: "The analogates are not similar." Both faces would be right. But because we use analogy to explore similarities between two realities, we tend to emphasize the face that says yes

rather than the one that says no. We need to keep in mind, however, that both faces are telling us truth. At times we need to look
at the "No" face to make sure that we do not forget that it really
is there in every analogy.

Now for an example. Suppose you have a friend whose name is
Bertha. She is married, has several children, and is deeply devoted
to her family. Nothing seems too much for her to do for her
husband and children. As a matter of fact, you might feel that
she carries her devotion too far. You might even say: "Bertha is
a slave to her family." Now when you say that you are using an
analogy. You are saying that there is something about Bertha that
is similar to what you think is true of a slave. Slaves belong to
their master in the totality of their life: their actions, their time,
their movements are all in the master's control. Bertha appears to
be similar to the slave in that she seems to belong so totally to
her family. To put it in the technical language I have suggested
above: Bertha and the slave are the analogates and "belonging
totally to another (or others)" is the analogon. So, one face of
the "analogon" will say: "Bertha and the slave are similar." But
it surely ought to be very clear that there are many significant
differences between Bertha and the slave. The slaves belong totally
to their master, not by choice but by a necessity imposed on them.
Bertha's total gift of herself to her family, on the other hand, is
a free decision that she makes herself. It is not necessity but love
and unselfish dedication that move her to spend herself for her
husband and children. Hence the "No" face of the "analogon"
would have to say: "Bertha and the slave are not similar."

The Negative Face of Analogy

The danger, as I have already suggested, in using analogy, is the
tendency to hear only the "Yes" face of the "analogon," since
we employ analogy precisely because we are trying to locate similarities. Hence, as a precaution — lest analogy mislead instead of
assist us in speaking about our experiences of God — we must, on
occasion at least, make a deliberate effort to hear from the other
face of the "analagon" (the one that says: "No, the experiences
are not similar").

No one knew better of this negative aspect of the analogous
term than the great Rhineland mystic of the fourteenth century,
Meister Eckhart. In one of his sermons he chides people for saying

that God is wise! "You call God wise," Eckhart says, "but God is not wise; I am wiser than God." What he is saying to what undoubtedly must have been a baffled congregation is that the only wisdom we know is that which we see in other human persons. This may be, in some people at least, a very deep wisdom, but it is so far removed from the Divine Wisdom that it hardly makes sense to call it "wisdom" at all! There is something refreshing and ultimately illuminating in Eckhart's somewhat unusual way of speaking about God. In fact, it not only reminds us of the "No" face of analogy, it also highlights the fact that, when we use analogy to talk about God, we must augment "like" with "more." By this I mean that when we apply to God some attribute we see in creatures, we must always add: "But it means infinitely *more* than that in God. It must be said to exist in God in a supereminent degree." Adding "more" to "like" softens a bit — but only a bit — the forcefulness with which we have to say, "unlike."

The Kataphatic Way
"Like" (or the "Yes" face of analogy) and "unlike" (its "No" face) have given rise to two different theological ways of speaking about God. One is called the *kataphatic way*. Since the Greek word *kataphasis* means "affirmation," this way of talking about God is the "like" side of analogy, its bright face, if you will. In other words, the *kataphatic* way is the way of light: we talk about God by affirming of God all the perfections we see in creatures. We have experiences of goodness and justice and compassion and we say: God is like this; indeed, God is like this to the highest possible degree. The experiences of fatherhood, motherhood, truthfulness, joyfulness — which are our experiences as created beings — serve as windows whereby we can look through the created world to the reality of God. Our human experiences, therefore, help us to speak about God. But the *kataphatic* way can only tell us *about* God. It cannot reach God's inmost reality, God's very life. For no created symbol, however deeply experienced, can ever adequately mirror the very reality of God.

The Apophatic Way
That is why there has always been another way of "talking" about God: the way of silence and darkness. This is known as the *apophatic way*. The term derives from the Greek word *apopha-*

sis, which means negation or denial. This is the "unlike" side of analogy, its dark face. As we strive to speak about God, the time eventually comes when we realize that images and ideas and words will not do; in fact, we find them a hindrance to the deep knowledge of God. To quote Eckhart again, the Rhineland mystic offers this cryptic but salutary advice to would-be theologians: "Seek God so as never to find Him." For if we think that we have found God in our words and thoughts and definitions, it is not really God we have in our grasp, but simply our own faltering speech about the Mystery we must ever be seeking, but will never fully grasp. If, therefore, we wish to enter into the Mystery of God's own reality, we must go, bare-handed if you will (with all conceptual gloves removed), into the Darkness. We must put out the lights of the mind and enter into the Unknown. We must take the *apophatic way*. Thomas Merton has written that apophaticism

> concerns itself with the most fundamental datum of all faith — and one which is often forgotten: the God who has revealed Himself to us in His Word has revealed Himself as unknown in His intimate essence, for He is beyond all mere human vision. "You cannot see my face: no man can see me and live" (Exodus 33:20). (*Contemplation in a World of Action*, p. 185)

Merton never underestimated the value of the kataphatic approach to God: we need to approach God through the windows on divine reality that created experiences open to us. Yet he believed that this way to God could never be ultimate. The time comes when it must yield place to apophaticism.

> Now, while the Christian contemplative must certainly develop, by study, the theological understanding of concepts about God, he is called mainly to penetrate the wordless darkness and apophatic light of an experience beyond concepts.... Relinquishing every attempt to grasp God in limited human concepts, the contemplative's act of submission and faith attains to His presence as the ground of every human experience and His reality as the ground of being itself.

It is worth noting that in this passage Merton speaks of "the apophatic light," even though the apophatic way is the way of darkness. The mystical tradition abounds in such seemingly paradoxical expressions: "the dazzling darkness," "the dark light," etc. The reason is that there is real knowledge attained through the apophatic way (one knows by not-knowing — once again the paradoxical way of speaking); the problem is that this knowledge is not the kind that can be articulated in words and formulated in statements. Speaking about "knowing through not knowing" is simply a way of suggesting the frustration experienced in trying to use words to express what is beyond words.

To speak of the ultimacy of the apophatic way is not intended to engender a kind of mild despair about theological speech, but simply to sound a warning. So it would surely be a mistake to take the attitude that my speech about God will be so far from the Reality of God that there is no point in trying to say anything. Quite the contrary. There is much that has been said in the past and is being said in the present that can help me approach, with real insight and perception, the mystery of God. But God still remains preeminently mystery. And mystery is not a problem that we must set out to solve; it is rather an invitation to deeper and deeper insights into the Unfathomable.

The Names of God

It will, then, be helpful for us — as we strive to deepen our awareness of the Presence of God — to make use of the kataphatic way and to reflect on the way we make use of images and symbols, drawn from our human experience, to try to express our experience of God. One way of doing this is to ponder some of the names we give to God, especially some of the names we find in the Scriptures.

Several years ago I was fascinated by a Sufi book I read called *The Ninety-Nine Names of Allah*. In the Sufi tradition God has given the ninety-nine divine names to His/Her people, but the greatest name is hidden in the Koran (the sacred book of Islam). The reason God hid the truest name there was so that people would read the entire Koran to discover that name. Reading this book about the ninety-nine names of God fired me with the desire to do something even more ambitious. I thought of going through our Judaeo-Christian Scriptures to find 365 names of God, one for each day of the year. I started the book, but never really got much farther than a week of names. So I still have 358 to go! But thinking about the subject of such a book was an experience I found very profitable; and since that book will never come to birth, I would like to share some of the ideas that came to me as I was tentatively planning it.

One of the first things I did was to travel, via a Concordance, through the Bible and discover the frequency with which the "name" of God appears. Perhaps the most important occurrence of the "name" comes in the famous passage of Exodus 3 (a passage that helped shape the title of this book), in which God responds to Moses' request that God tell him the divine name so that he may communicate it to the people in Egypt.

> God said: "This is what you shall tell the Israelites: 'I AM [YHWH
> — the four consonants, whose meaning, as was discussed earlier,
> is uncertain] sent me to you.'"
>
> God spoke further to Moses: "Thus shall you say to the Is-
> raelites: 'The Lord [YHWH], the God of your ancestors, the God
> of Abraham, the God of Isaac, the God of Jacob has sent me to
> you.'
> > This is my *Name* forever;
> > this is my *Title* for all generations."

Moving on from this key passage, I located many wondrous references to the divine name scattered throughout the Bible, yet especially prominent perhaps in the Book of Psalms, which might well be described as a book of praise of the name of God.

> O Lord, Our Lord,
> How glorious is your *Name* over all the earth. (Ps. 8:2)
>
> They trust in you who cherish your *Name*,
> for you forsake not those who seek you, O Lord. (Ps. 9:11)
>
> Some are strong in chariots; some in horses;
> we are strong in the *Name* of the Lord. (Ps. 29:8)
>
> Give to the Lord glory and praise
> Give to the Lord the glory due his *Name*. (Ps. 29:1–2)
>
> O God, by your *Name* save me,
> and by your might defend my cause. (Ps. 54:3)
>
> The nations shall revere your *Name*, O Lord,
> and all the kings of the earth your glory. (Ps. 102:16)

Our help is in the *Name* of the Lord,
who made heaven and earth. (Ps. 124: 8)

Praise the Lord, for the Lord is good;
sing praise to his *Name*, which we love. (Ps. 135: 3)

The *Name* of the Lord is a strong tower;
the just person runs to it and is safe. (Prov. 18: 10)

Yes, for your ways and your judgments, O Lord,
we look to you;
your *Name* and your *Title* are the desire of our souls. (Isa. 26: 8)

This is but a brief sampling of the numerous references to God's name that run through the pages of Scripture. What I should like to do now is to consider some of the *specific names* — the metaphorical and symbolic terms drawn from our own experience — that we make use of as we strive to talk about God. One might say that these metaphors and symbols are like so many "vowels" that we add to the four consonants (YHWH) in order that we may say something about our God whose *proper* name is unpronounceable (for it has come down to us only as consonants) and unknowable (since its original meaning has been lost in history).

What kind of symbols do we employ kataphatically to speak about God? As I look over the notes of the irrevocably abandoned book on the 365 names of God, I notice that I made a distinction between what I was going to call "our names" and "my names." Our names are community names, names that arise out of the life of a people experiencing the Saving Presence of God in that history. They form the cherished heritage of that people. Because they are the common property of a community of faith, they may be used even by those who may not have shared the original experience, but who do share the life of the community. It must be said, however, that when a community's history changes radically, this may mean that the symbols that spoke in past circumstances cease to carry meaning in a situation that is new and markedly different.

When I use the term "my names," I am speaking about a way of naming God that rises out of an individual's existential experience of God's Presence — an experience that evokes a response. (Obviously I use the term "my," not to designate the author of this book, but any *individual* as distinguished from the *community* of faith.) For the most part these names express a here-and-now encounter with God.

"Our names" of God are the names used by a people who became aware of God's Presence in their history and constructed the Bible out of that history. "My names" of God (at least those that come out of the Scriptures) are God's gifts to those who construct their lives out of the Bible and the challenges it offers. While our names are ways of identifying God, my names are a way in which we identify ourselves with God. Our names one can know simply by reading the Bible: a person can know them without necessarily becoming involved. But my names are different: I cannot simply read them in the Bible; I have to discover them there. I discover them only when I experience them. I might put it in this way: our names are nouns that were once verbs (when the actual experience happened that they name); my names are verbs. By this I mean they speak of God's action in my life here and now. Once we have experienced God's action in our lives (God's action as verb), we can articulate that experience in a noun.

To offer an example, there is, in Psalm 54, a quaint expression that suggests that God's loving regard for us is so great that God carefully collects all our tears in a bottle. Thus the psalm:

> My wanderings you have counted;
> my tears are stored in your flask;
> are they not recorded in your book?

Anyone can read this verse and admire its poetic beauty; but only the one who experiences being so loved and cared for by God can be moved by the experience and, eventually, turn the experience into a noun that names God: "The-One-who-stores-my-tears-in-His-flask." Again, a person may read Psalm 9:

> They trust in you who cherish your name,
> for you forsake not those who seek you, O Lord.

But only the person who has known God's protection and love can turn this verse into a name for God: The-One-Who-never-forsakes-those-who-seek-Her."

The names of God are many. We need only to read the Bible to discover them: God is our Savior, Redeemer, and Deliverer. God is our Strength, our Rock, our Shield, our Stronghold, our Fortress, our Helper, our Refuge, our Vindicator. God is King, Ruler, and Lord of hosts. God is Father, Mother, Lover, Husband. God is Friend. God is Shepherd, Protector and Guardian, the Father of orphans and the Defender of widows. God is the Builder and the Vine-dresser. God is the Holy One. God is Judge of all.

These are the names we can discover simply by reading the Bible and listening to its words. Then there are the never-to-be-enumerated names that individual persons are able to give to God as they read the Bible and react to the God who here and now speaks through its pages and calls all of us to respond.

We have been talking about various kataphatic terms we may use to talk about God. If we reflect on the names we have given to God — all of them rising out of our own human experience — we can see that all of them are relational: we relate to God as the One who is our Source and Sustainer, the One who cares for us and provides for us. All of which is to say that we are talking about a God who loves us, or, to use Merton's words, the God who is the "Hidden Ground of Love."

When we call God "Love" or "the Hidden Ground of Love," we are drawing on a human experience: we all, hopefully, love and are loved. Yet love is the deepest of all human mysteries. We can experience it, but we cannot really describe what it is that we are experiencing. We can say things about it — and poets through the centuries have done so with great passion. But nothing we say can really tell us what love is in itself.

Love: Bridge between the Kataphatic and Apophatic Ways

Love, therefore, becomes a bridge between the two ways of speaking about God. Because we are, finally, in the darkness when we try to speak about love and have to listen to what our hearts say, Love, which at first blush appears to be a kataphatic way of talking about God, leads us into the apophatic way. For the apophatic way takes leave of the mind in which words arise that want to reason about God and turns to the heart, which alone can contain God whom the whole world cannot contain. As Merton writes in one of his journals: "The heart only is capable of knowing God."

It is the only place strong enough to bear the divine secret: the secret of who God is.

That *God loves us* is, I believe, the wondrous truth that we need to keep saying to ourselves and to all who will listen to us. It is something that Scripture, especially the New Testament, is soaked in. I touched briefly on this in chapter 3 and also in chapter 4 and want to discuss it now in more detail: the approach that is summed up in the First Epistle of John, where he says: "God is Love." This notion of God should be at the heart of our own praying, the spiritual direction that is offered to people, the homilies that are preached from our pulpits. For me it is the essential affirmation of the New Testament. It is *the* text of the Bible that I find hermeneutically decisive. By that I mean that it is the text that becomes the key for understanding everything else in Scripture. And I find support for my choice of this as the decisive text in the great fifteenth chapter of Luke. Its three parables (the caring shepherd, the happy woman who finds her lost coin, the prodigal son and his loving father) are at the center of his Gospel and carry its central message. And there is Paul's magnificent poem on love as the heart of the Christian life in the thirteenth chapter of 1 Corinthians. Paul puts it quite simply: If we have everything but not love, then in reality we have nothing.

Surely to say that God is "Love," is not to resolve the mystery of God. It is rather, as I have already suggested, to touch the mystery of God with another mystery. For Love itself is as incomprehensible as God. Yet we have experiences of love in our lives. These experiences can help us to understand a little more clearly who God is.

I believe we have to emphasize this truth as so absolutely central to the Gospel, because so many people tend to see our God as a God of moral sanctions. God is seen as a God of rewards and punishments, almost as if this were God's only reason for being. This false and illusory notion of God, which all too many people share in to a greater or lesser degree, sees God as someone who is gracious to me when I am good, but who punishes me relentlessly when I am bad. This is a typical patriarchal notion of God. *He* is the God of Noah who sees people deep in sin, repents that He made them and resolves to destroy them. *He* is the God of the desert who sends snakes to bite His people because they murmured against Him. *He* is the God of David who practically decimates a people, because their King — motivated by pride perhaps — takes up a census of his empire. *He* is the God who exacts the last drop of blood from His Son, so that His just anger, evoked by sin, may be appeased. This God whose moods alternate between graciousness and fierce anger — a God who is still all too familiar to many Christians — is a caricature of the true God. This God does not exist. This is not the God whom Jesus Christ reveals to us. This is not the God whom Jesus called "Abba."

John the Baptist Imprisoned

One of the most distressing scenes in the Gospels is that of John the Baptist in Herod's prison. Weak, lonely, depressed, he seems almost to have lost the ability to hope in the future. Yet it was not his own future that concerned him. (He could well anticipate what that might be. Not many of Herod's prisoners emerged from prison alive.) It was the future of the mission he had begun. His life had been dedicated to preparing the way for the One-Who-Was-to-Come. When Jesus appeared on the scene, he was confident that Jesus was that One. But now, in the terrible misery of his prison cell, he is not so sure. For Jesus was not acting like the Messiah. He was not saying what the Messiah was supposed to be saying. John is forced to face the agonizing possibility that would make his whole life a question mark: "Had he picked the wrong candidate?"

Classical Prophetism vs. Jesus' Preaching

John found himself forced to question the very *raison d'être* of his life. For, following in the line of all the prophets of Israel, he had called the people to repentance. Like all the prophets he had preached: Repent or *else*. Repent or you will surely experience the wrath of God. This was classical prophetic teaching. It's what John had to say. It is what he expected Jesus to say.

His problem was that Jesus was not saying this. True, Jesus was calling people to repent, to mend their ways; and in this he was in harmony with the voice of prophetism. But Jesus' call to repentance was followed, not by the classical "or," but by a wholly different "and." He did not say: Repent *or* God will punish you. His message was totally different: "Repent *and* then you will be able to see the love and mercy of God that has always been extended to you."

This was *not just a difference of emphasis in preaching*. It was preaching that was saying something totally different about God. The prophets' message was *that God's love is conditional*. God will love you *on the condition that you behave*. Because that condition is always there and because human persons are often so very weak, the prophetic picture of God inevitably comes out as the picture of a God of wrath. And equally inevitably the basic human stance toward God, in the light of that message, will be fear. When I am conscious of my sinfulness and weakness (and who of us is not?), then *a God whose love is conditional scares me*.

John, reflecting in the darkness of his prison cell, had heard enough about Jesus' preaching to know that he was saying something quite different. Jesus said what no prophet before him had dared to say. He had said that *God's love was unconditional*. In Jesus' preaching, there was no room for "God loves you, if..." His preaching was quite simply: "God loves you." This is the problem John was brooding about. Maybe he thought it too good to be true — what Jesus was preaching. Or maybe his mind was so locked into the traditional beliefs about God that he was scarcely free to believe the GOOD NEWS that Jesus brought.

Notice how Jesus activates John's freedom to change his thinking. He does not try to alter John's thinking by a command. (This, I might add in parenthesis, is a mistake all too commonly made by authority: thinking that a command to accept something, especially if it is repeated often enough, can get people to change their minds. This is impossible: the way one thinks cannot be the object of a command.) Jesus does not say to John: "Look here. You must believe what I say because I say it."

No, Jesus' method of persuasion is simply to tell John to look at the facts. Look at what God is doing through me among his people. Take account of your experience and the experience of others you know. Note how God is giving sight to the blind, hearing to the deaf, and strong limbs to the crippled. But what is more important than all of these is that the Good News is being preached to the special objects of God's love: the poor. And the Good News is that God is Love, not Wrath.

What Jesus is saying to John is this: "All your life you have been brought up to think about God in one particular way. I am calling you to change your thinking. But I invite you to do this by looking at what people are actually experiencing about God. Then, in the light of that experience, be free enough in your own heart to think differently about God. Or, to put it another way, let the truth about God set you free. Don't let that truth be a stumbling block to you because it appears to be new."

What was John's reaction to the message Jesus sent him? Did he accept the Good News and go to his martyr's death in peace? We do not know, as this is one of many tantalizing stories, so frequent in the Gospels, where we are left cliff-hanging and not informed of what happened next. It may well be that the story is left incomplete because it is not just John's story, but the story of each one of us. Like John, we have to be ready to experience what God is doing in our world. We have to be prepared to accept God as "Unconditional Love." And once we do this, we have to ask what this means about the way we must choose to live our lives. (See chapter 4 above.)

Sincere followers of Jesus who have an image of God that does not square with Jesus' preaching need help to deal with that image and rid themselves of it. They must be led to an understanding of what it means to speak of God as "the Hidden Ground of Love." In his book *Seasons of Celebration*, Merton laments the fact that so many who profess to love God seem to be unsure whether or not that love is reciprocated. Too often they regard God, he says, "as a furious Father who seeks only to punish and revenge Himself for the evil that is done 'against Him.'" This is a false God. This is not the Father of our Lord Jesus Christ who is also our Father — and our Mother.

It is true that there are *hard* passages in the Hebrew Bible that seem to present an angry God. But we need to remember that the biblical revelation of God is only gradual and reaches its fullest possibility only in Jesus Christ. The Hebrew Scriptures, which tell us that God made human beings in the divine image, often seem to make their God in their own image. Many of the problems about God in the Hebrew Scriptures disappear when we realize that people often projected their own notions on God. We have to correct the anthropomorphisms of the Hebrew Bible and complete, through Jesus, the partial and gradual revelation of God that is there.

When we do so, we find that the whole Bible is the story of God accepting us, not because we deserve it, not because we are sinless, but because God is God: the Hidden Ground of Love in all that He/She has made. Karl Barth expressed it so strikingly when he said: God deals with us not with a natural *therefore*, but with a miraculous *nevertheless*. The sequence is not: we are unworthy, *therefore* God rejects us; but rather, we are unworthy, *nevertheless* God accepts us.

Thomas Merton makes the same point. He sees in the human tendency to cringe before a God of vengeance a projection of our own need to feel worthy, coupled with the uneasy feeling that we are in fact unworthy. We look for goodness in ourselves that might move God to love us; and failing to find it, we fear God as "a tremendous and insatiable power who *needs to see goodness* in us and who, for all the clarity of His vision, finds nothing but evil and therefore insists upon revenge." Such an attitude prevents us, Merton says, from having an authentic experience of God. For, as he points out:

> One of the keys to real religious experience is the shattering realization that no matter how hateful we are to ourselves, we are not hateful to God. This realization helps us to understand the difference between our love and His. Our love is a need, His a gift. We need to see good in ourselves in order to love ourselves. He does not. He loves us not because we are good, but because He is. (*The New Man*, p. 96)

On March 8, 1966, Merton wrote to an Anglican woman with whom he had been corresponding: "You say you don't think you love God and that is probably perfectly true. But what matters is that God loves you, isn't it? If we had to rely on our love, where would we be?"

Merton also writes: "The root of Christian love is not the will to love, but *the faith that one is loved*. The faith that one is loved *by God*. The faith that one is loved by God although unworthy — or rather, irrespective of one's worth."

In *Seasons of Celebration*, he says: "It is not and cannot be Love's will to be severe and punish." Our God is not a vengeful God. Rather God is like "a calm sea of mercy. In Him there is no anger. He is not severe, and it is not theologically accurate to say that He becomes angry, that He is moved to hurt and punish" (p. 120).

Some years ago I gave a talk in one of the parishes of the diocese of Rochester. I have no remembrance of the topic. But a long time afterward, I met a woman who had been at the talk. She told me that she had walked out of the church hall that evening with an older woman. The older woman said to her: "Father's talk was very important to me. For the first time in my life I feel that it is possible for me to be saved." My first reaction was: I wish I could remember what I had said. But also I thought: how sad that this woman had gone all through her life, probably living as a reasonably good Christian, but never really believing that in the end all would be all right for her.

In the Gospel of St. Thomas Jesus is reported as saying: "the one who is near me is near the Fire." That Fire is God's Love that purifies us and, once we are cleansed of all that is alien to It, the Fire consumes us so that we become as it were indistinguishable from the Fire, finding our identity in It and, in the finding of our own identity, coming to know the Fire Itself.

We shall find that Fire only if we look first within ourselves. Or, if I may paraphrase the words of Meister Eckhart again: If you look outside yourself, you will never find God. But if you look within yourself, you will discover God. And you will discover God *not only there, but everywhere*. "I shall walk in the Presence of the Lord in the land of the living." "May I experience the Joy of Life in your Presence."

A FOOTNOTE TO CHAPTER SEVEN: INCLUSIVE LANGUAGE

Earlier in this chapter I said that "all the knowledge we have of God comes from some human experience of God." Human experience means the experience of women and men. Yet it is a regrettable fact that, until very recently, most of our theology seemed to suggest that it was male experience rather than total human experience that helped us to know God and to attempt to name God. Theology, again until recently, has described God as male and has used exclusively male terms to describe the human experience of God. Male terms have also dominated the vocabulary of prayer. When we wanted to pray for all of humanity, we prayed for "all men."

There are those who would use linguistic arguments to justify such exclusive language. They would say that in Greek, for instance, there is a term *anthropos*, which designated the whole human species (*aner* is the Greek word for the male person); likewise, in Latin *homo* means humanity, and another word (*vir*) designates the male. English, so the argument goes, lacks the luxuriance of distinguishing gender words that one finds in the classical languages. But *it has always been understood* that the term "men" is intended to designate both men and women. Hence when we pray for "all men," we intend to include women also. Or when we talk about the way "men" experience God, we are talking about women's experience as well.

This argument is open to serious challenge. For when we talk about the way in which the term "men" has always been understood, we are really talking about the way in which it has been understood by men (males). Women, until quite recently, have had very little say in the matter, because the culture that claims this understanding of "men" is a culture that had been paternalistic, male-dominated, and oppressive of women. Moreover, it has presumed to validate its use of exclusive language by making use of only male terms and male pronouns to describe the deity.

Since this book is about the prayer of awareness and not about the sexism that characterizes our culture, I have no intention of attempting to defend what I have just said about the male domination of our culture and of an important symbol of that culture, its language. Those who agree with the position I have stated need no argument; those who disagree would probably be unconvinced by any defense I might try to present. This may well be one of those situations I had in mind when I spoke, in chapter 6, about the need at times for creative waiting for awareness, though even as I say this I am all too aware of the increasing number of women today who would want to say: "We have waited long enough. Now is the time to act — for justice and equality."

I bring up the exclusive-inclusive language debate, because it belongs in a chapter entitled "Talking about God." Generally it is possible, with a bit of circumlocution and something of creativity, to avoid exclusive terms where general human experiences, common to women and men, are being talked about. What really taxes one's ingenuity is avoiding the constant use of exclusively male symbols to describe God. It seems that, in the Church I belong to — for too many members at least — God is "Caucasian, male, and Roman Catholic." I suppose there might even be those who would want to add that God is "American."

Certainly, the experience of fatherhood is a human experience common to men and women that can be used as a symbol to describe God. Hence it is perfectly legitimate to call God "Father," especially when we have in mind the word that Jesus used for "Father," the word "Abba." "Abba" is a term of endearment addressed to one who does not dominate, but who loves tenderly. But having said this we need to add two qualifications. First, the term "Father" is so often used, not in the sense of "Abba," but as a justification for an institutional structure in religion that is male-dominated. Second, and more important, there is another phenomenon, as common to men and women as the experience of "father," and that is the experience of "mother." There are insights into God that come from the symbol of "mother" that we could never learn from the symbol of "father" alone. Hence it is not just feminist thinking; it is good theology to call God "Mother." Symbols of the deity function in theology to complement and even to correct one another. Indeed, to use one symbol to the exclusion of all others is to turn that symbol into an idol. A mental image can be as idolatrous as a graven one.

Other problems about God-language arise from images in the Scriptures that are male, without any female counterpart. Thus, there are the images that speak of power: King, Lord, Master, and such like. Probably most problematic of all is the question: how does one respect a commitment to avoiding the exclusive use of male terms and still use pronouns to refer to God? Take such a simple notion as the love God has for people. Do you say: "God loves *His* people" or "God loves *Her* people" or "God loves *His/Her* people" or "God loves God's people"? Or do you try to alternate all four modes of expression?

My inclination during the writing of this book up to this point was to use the last two forms: the last as often as possible, the third, where it seems too ponderous to repeat the name of God once again. Just before writing this footnote to this chapter, I invited a colleague (a woman professor of religious studies) to read the first six chapters of this book's typescript. She found the frequent use of His/Her heavy and even distracting and suggested more frequent repetition of the term "God." This is what I have tried to do in the final revision. I do not find this a completely satisfactory solution. But while I (and others too) search for better ways of handling this issue, I do want to make clear my own strong commitment to the use of inclusive language. If this means that writing at times becomes a bit awkward, it's a small price to pay, by way of reparation, for the rampant sexism that in the past has colored so much of our theological writing.

8

Who Am I?
My Search for the True Me

"The happiness of being at one with everything
in that Hidden Ground of Love."
(Thomas Merton)

Several years ago a woman in England, who had been corresponding with me about Thomas Merton and her interest in his works,
wrote that her sister who had been very close to her had died
and that she was sad and depressed. I tried in a number of letters to offer her some help and consolation. As an introduction
to this chapter "Who Am I?" I would like to quote, with her
permission, from one of these letters:

> I hope you have been able to come to grips a bit more with your
> feelings about your sister's death. I realize how very hard this is
> for you. You need to keep reflecting on the fact that, while in one
> sense death separates us from loved ones, in another and more ul-
> timate sense it deepens our spiritual union with them. When there
> is only *that*, then *that* becomes most important. And of course it
> should really be most important at all times. We are one with one
> another, because whatever of us there is that is really worthwhile is
> from God and in God. And that is something that death does not
> and cannot change — though it appears to do so, since we are so
> accustomed to think of a person solely in terms of her empirical
> ego. Death is the end of the empirical ego, but not of the person.
> We are all eternally one in the love of God.

I begin with this concrete narrative of the death of a loved
one and some reflections I offered on the meaning of that death,
because in this chapter I want to deal with the question of self-

identity. This book is about the prayer of awareness. Having written about the God of whom we are aware, I need now to offer some thoughts on the "I" who is aware of God. Total awareness of the Presence of God is the final answer to my prayer: "May I experience the Joy of Life in your Presence." But who is that "I" who desires and eventually achieves this joy in the Holy Presence? Remember that I have stated quite emphatically that it would be a wrong understanding of wordless prayer to think that I as a separate subject become aware of God as a separate Object. In various way I have tried to make clear that God and I are not separate. God and I are not two, but one. Apart from God I am nothing. Or, as I expressed it in the letter, "Whatever of us there is that is really worthwhile is from God and in God."

If you are wondering, a bit nervously (after all, these days one never knows when the Grand Inquisitor in whatever guise may be looking over one's shoulder), whether this seems to smack of pantheism or even appears to suggest that God and I are one, my unabashed answer is: "Of course, it does." But the reason is not because I believe in pantheism or think that I am God, but because I am trying to describe in dualistic terms a reality that can only be understood nondualistically. Perhaps we could go back once again to a text I have referred to at least twice so far: Merton's words to the Smith College students. What he says to them, in effect, is:

(1) Awareness ("attentiveness" is the word he uses) opens the door to happiness.

(2) It does so precisely because (a) it pushes us beyond the dualities that life seems to press upon us and (b) it gives us the consciousness of "being at one with everything."

(3) Yet this oneness with everything that generates happiness is no pantheistic or impersonal melange. For it is rooted in a Hidden Ground; and that Ground is personal, for it is the "Ground of Love." This happiness that springs from the experience of "oneness" is something I find when I find God; for, in a Christian context at least, the Hidden Ground of Love is God. When I truly experience God my subjectivity becomes one with the subjectivity of God; I experience not separateness but oneness; and it is in this oneness with God that I come to experience my oneness within myself (my own identity) and my oneness with my sisters and brothers and with all else that is. This oneness, with the love

and compassion it calls forth and the creative energy and selfless giving it engenders, constitutes true human happiness. It is the recovery of the original blessing of self-identity experienced in total awareness.

Writing to Mark Van Doren on October 16, 1954, Merton tells of a book of his that was soon to be published, called *The New Man*. Merton summarizes its contents:

> It is about the business of "coming to oneself" and "awakening" out of the inexistential torpor that most people live in, and finding one's real identity in God.... Our knowledge of Him is no longer merely as though it were the knowledge of an "object"! (Who could bear such a thing; and yet religious people do it: just as if the world contained here a chair, there a house, there a hill and then again God. *As though the identity of all were not hidden in Him Who has no name.* (*The Road to Joy*, Farrar Straus and Giroux, 1989; italics added)

At this point, you may be inclined to say: I have a problem. All this sounds quite wonderful. I would like to believe that it is true; and the strange thing is that there are times in my life when it even seems that it ought to be true. Yet, generally speaking, I have to say that it does not seem to square with my ordinary experience. I seem to have a strong consciousness of things in separateness rather than in oneness. More than that, I'm not sure that I have any real experience of my own identity, let alone my "identity hidden in Him Who has no name." For sure, I very much want to know my own identity. I have, moreover, a strong feeling (which I cannot explain) that it is there for the discovering. But so far this hasn't happened to me, though I have the feeling in my bones that this is what religion and faith, in the long run, are all about.

Original Blessing

This problem, together with the insight it embodies, is something many people could say "amen" to; for it mirrors their experience. Indeed, it embodies an intuition shared by many of the high religions that the happiness that all women and men *now* seek is actually a reality that they have lost, but that they possessed *in the beginning*. The *original blessing* given to humanity (often represented as the paradisal state) was nothing other than the gift of self-awareness or the experience of one's own identity. Zen Buddhists call it the experience of "your original face before you were born."

Original Blessing as Cosmic Dance
In the final chapter of *New Seeds of Contemplation* Thomas Merton has some moving poetic prose that describes this original blessing as the "cosmic dance." What does he mean by the "cosmic dance"? It is really another way of saying what he described in the Smith College letter: that at-oneness-with-everything. The cosmic dance is the universe, the cosmos God made, moving in perfect harmony with the Creator. This harmonious oneness with God was God's original gift to creation and especially to the man and the woman in that creation. God made the man and the woman in God's own image, so that, through the light of reason, they might know all the other creatures and give them their names (and that naming is actually "recorded" in Genesis 2). But that was not all. God also gave them a higher light that goes beyond names and forms, a light through which God's human creatures are able to meet God, not through the medium of things, but in God's own simplicity. "The union of the simple light of God," Merton says, "with the simple light of [the human] spirit, in love, is contemplation." For Merton, then, the original blessing was contemplation. He goes on:

> The two simplicities are one. They form, as it were, an *emptiness* in which there is no addition, but rather the taking away of names, of forms, of content, of subject matter, of identities. [That is, of "identities" that do not truly identify because they isolate us from the Ground in which alone we have being. —note added] In this meeting there is not so much a fusion of entities as a disappearance of entities.

Once again making the link with the beginnings of Genesis, Merton says:

> The Bible speaks of this very simply: "In the breeze after noon, God came to walk with Adam [and Eve] in Paradise." ... In the free *emptiness* of the breeze God and [God's human creatures] are together, not speaking in words or syllables or forms. And that was the meaning of creation, and of Paradise.

In that *emptiness* that knows no dualities, but only the oneness of simplicity, the walk of God with human creatures in unison and tranquil accord is poetry, not prose. That is to say it is the dance. For what is dance but harmonious movement in perfect oneness and beyond all dualities and multiplicities? In the dance there are not many movements, but one movement. The dancers forget themselves: they lose themselves in the dance and thus are emptied of any separate self. And it is in that emptiness that the movement of the dance goes on.

Yet when God created us, God made us free. We have a choice. We can be a self that refuses to lose itself in the dance — which means that we are unwilling to rise above the dualities that illusion projects on reality. Or we can be a self that is aware of its nonseparateness and of its oneness with all of reality and with its Divine Source. And when we are aware of this true self — which is emptiness, for it *is* only in God — then, in all truth, we belong to the dance. To put it in Merton's words: "If we could let go of our own obsession with what we think is the meaning of it all, we might be able to hear His call and follow Him in His mysterious cosmic dance."

> We do not have to go very far to catch echoes...of that dancing. When we are alone on a starlit night; when by chance we see the migrating birds in autumn descending on a grove of junipers to rest and eat; when we see children in a moment when they are really children; when we know love in our hearts; or when, like the Japanese poet Basho, we hear an old frog land in a quiet pond with a solitary splash — at such times the awakening, the turning inside out of all values, the "newness," the emptiness and the purity of vision that make themselves evident, provide a glimpse of the cosmic dance. (*New Seeds of Contemplation*, pp. 296–97)

Original Sin

Though there is in most of the high religions this intuition that the original blessing (call it paradisal existence or the cosmic dance or the primal experience of contemplative oneness) was "in the beginning," and is still there for us to catch echoes of, there is also this other deeply felt intuition: the realization that this is not the way things appear to be. Participation in the cosmic dance is not what we ordinarily experience. *Original blessing* has been lost and its place taken by *original sin*. Original sin embodies the intuition: "I am not what I ought to be"; or, put more mysteriously: "I am not what I appear to be." Thus the myth of paradise (the "place" of the original blessing) has yielded to the myth of the fall (the experience of original sin). The harmony of creation seems to have disappeared and, except for fleeting glimpses, exists only in memory. The "fall" is the name we give to the puzzling and inexplicable fact that we experience ourselves as alienated from the cosmic dance, despoiled of the sense of our own identity, and cut off from the state of contemplation. When we speak of the fall as original *sin*, we are using the term "sin" analogically: it expresses the existential reality of our alienation from God and creation, without attempting to assign to any one in particular the blame or responsibility for this alienation.

While we may have difficulty in explaining how this alienation came about, we have no difficulty in experiencing that it is there. There seems to be an abyss separating us from God and from our own true self and God's good creation.

Enter the False Self

Why is it that what we actually experience is so different from what it would seem we ought to be experiencing? In a word, why do we experience original sin instead of original blessing? If we look for the villain in the story, that role — according to Merton's thinking — would be played by the false self. At this point I need to warn the unwary reader that this term, as Merton uses it, is somewhat elusive and difficult to understand. I confess to struggling with it for a long time and finding myself still a bit diffident about offering my present view of what it means. It surely is a term that can easily be misinterpreted. Thus one could easily make the mistake of reading it in *a moral sense*, in which case, one would be inclined to think of the "false self" as being untruthful, sinful, immoral. Now there is no doubt that it can, and perhaps often does, mean that. But, as I see it, such a meaning is *derivative* and does not catch the primary sense in which Merton uses the term "false self." In speaking of the *false* self, Merton, if I understand him correctly, is thinking primarily in ontological terms. By this I mean that the adjective "false" conveys the notion of unsubstantiality, of lacking in any fullness of being. The "false self" is, one might say, deficient in being: deficient especially in the sense that it is impermanent, not enduring. It cannot survive death. To put it colloquially: it doesn't amount to much.

That "false self" has primarily this ontological meaning for Merton is borne out, I think, by reflection on other adjectives he often uses as substitutes for "false," for example, "external," "superficial," "empirical," "outward," "contingent," "private," "shadow," "illusory," "fictitious," "smoke," "feeble," "petty." All these adjectives suggest, in different ways, that we are dealing with a self that is real, but only at a very limited level of reality. The false self keeps us on the surface of reality: both its fears and its joys are superficial. It is limited *by* time and space and *to* time and space: it has a biography and a history, both of which we write by the actions we perform and the roles we play and both of which are destined to cease with death. That is why Merton calls it "the evanescent self" or the "smoke self" that will disappear like smoke up a chimney. Its well-being needs constantly to be fed by accomplishments and by the admiration and affirmation of others. It is the ego-self, the self as object or, in Merton's words:

> the self which we observe as it goes about its biological business, the machine which we regulate and tune up and feed with all kinds of stimulants and sedatives, constantly trying to make it run more and more smoothly, to fit the patterns prescribed by the salesman of pleasure-giving and anxiety-laden commodities. (*Faith and Violence*, p. 112)

Salvation: Death and Rebirth

What must we do to move beyond this empirical ego, which alienates us from our true being, and recover that true and substantial self that is beyond and above the level of mere empirical individuality with its superficial enjoyments and fears? The Christian answer (and there are similar answers in other religions) is that there must be death and rebirth. To quote Merton again:

> In order to become one's true self, the false self must die. In order for the inner self to appear the outer self must disappear: or at least become secondary, unimportant. . . .
> True Christianity is growth in the life of the Spirit, a deepening of the new life, a continuous rebirth, in which the exterior and superficial life of the ego-self is discarded like an old snake skin

and the mysterious invisible self of the Spirit becomes more present and more active. (*Love and Living*, p. 199)

This growth involves an ongoing transformation, whereby we are liberated from selfishness and grow in love so that, in some sense, we become love or, once again in the words of the Smith College text, we are "at one with everything in that Hidden Ground of Love," which we can only experience but never explain. We die to selfishness and come alive in love.

How is this blessing achieved, whereby we are able finally to transcend the empirical self and discover, once and for all, our true self? Thomas Merton's answer, I believe, would be that this consummation occurs either in death or in contemplation, which is to say that it is either an eschatological experience or an in-depth prayer experience that transforms my consciousness.

Most people, he would say, arrive at this full awakening of the true self only in death. For death is better understood, not as the separation of the soul from the body, but as the disappearance of the false self and the emergence of the true self. Seen not as a passion (namely, something that happens to a person), but as an action (i.e., something that a person does), death is the moment of the fullest human freedom. In that moment, freed from the limitations of space and time, we are able to cast aside the illusions that once were so captivating, and in an emptiness hitherto unexperienced are enabled at last to affirm our true identity. We die into God. We discover in death what was always true, but not adverted to, that we are in God. Death is being in the Hidden Ground of Love in full attentive awareness. This is eternal happiness: the return to the original blessing.

This side of that eschatological awakening, it is possible to realize one's true self only in the experience of contemplation. Contemplation is the highest form of the "spiritual life." It means that one is totally empty (i.e., of all separateness) and at the same time totally full (i.e., at one with all that is and with the Source and Ground of all). In contemplation

the infinitely "fontal" (source-like) creativity of our being in Being is somehow attained and becomes in its turn a source of action and creativity in the world around us. (*Faith and Violence*, p. 115)

How absurd, then, to think — as some people do — that contemplation has to do with God to the exclusion of all else: as if God were an "Object" that must be preferred to "all other objects." In *A Vow of Conversation* Merton reflects on the

> unutterable confusion of those who think that God is a mental object and that to "love God alone" is to exclude all other objects and concentrate on this one. Fatal. Yet that is why so many misunderstand the meaning of contemplation. (P. 142)

The discovery of the true self — whether in contemplation or in death — is the termination of the experience of duality. More than that it is the end of dualistic speech. At this point it seems proper for me to repeat the admission I made near the beginning of this chapter that the principal difficulty in writing this chapter, not to say in reading it, is that the language we speak rises out of the experience of duality. The language of nondualism is silence: a communing that is beyond words and beyond thoughts. One of the problems I have experienced in writing this chapter, indeed the whole book, is that so often I have had to put words on silence. I have been obliged to describe nondualism with terms that are dualistic. Almost inevitably this means that I have given an impression that I do not intend to convey: namely (in this instance, for example), the notion that when I talk about the "true self" and the "false self" there is somehow a third party who *has* these "two" selves and in whom "they" battle to see who wins out.

I will mention just two examples. Early in the chapter I said that there seems to be an abyss "*separating us* from our true self"; and, later, something similar: "The false self keeps *us* on the surface of reality." The obvious question that comes to a perceptive reader is: whom are we designating when we speak of the "us separated from our true self" or the "us kept on the surface of reality"? And, lest you think that it is I who am muddling language, let me cite yet another example of this dualistic writing, but this time from one of Merton's works. In his book *The Wisdom of the Desert*, he speaks of the spiritual journey of the Fathers of the Egyptian desert: an inner journey more important, he believes, than any flight into outer space. For Merton asks, "What can we gain by sailing to the moon, if we are not able to cross the abyss that separates us from ourselves?" (p. 11). What he is saying is that we have to cross the abyss that separates our surface consciousness from the deep and creative realm of the unconscious. Only when we cross over do we become our true self. At this point, dualistic language simply breaks down. For if my true self is on the other side of the abyss, who is it that crosses over that abyss? I simply cannot give an answer to this koan-like question. There is no real crossing over. For the true self simply is. And that is it. As Merton once expressed it: "You have to experience duality for a long time until you see it's not there" (David Steindl-Rast, "Recollections of Thomas Merton's Last Days in the West," *Monastic Studies*, September 1969).

What this makes clear (Do I hear you saying: "At this point I would not advise you to use the word 'clear'"?) is that the only possible direct approach to our true self, as to God, is the apophatic way. Like our experience of God, our experience of the true self is noetic and ineffable: we know what we did not know before, but what we know is inexpressible and ineffable. This is simply to say that the true self is not an object that is accessible to our rational processes. You will never get to know your real self by reading what I write about it (and do I hear a voice agreeing: "You can say that again"?) For the real self is our own subjectivity that can never be known as an object or a thing. I cannot "see" my true self any more than I can see my own eyes.

In contemplative prayer I become *aware* of myself, not by an act of reasoning, but rather by an act of intuition that is beyond the duality of subject and object. For this experience of my *Inner Self* is an experience of my total and radical dependence on God. Hence it is an experience of God on whom I am totally and radically dependent. It would be wrong to think that we are talking about two different experiences. No, it is one and the same intuition in which I experience God and find my own identity in God. When I find God I find my deepest self. Merton puts this well in *The Climate of Monastic Prayer:* "Our knowledge of God is paradoxically a knowledge not of Him as the object of our scrutiny, but of ourselves as utterly dependent on His saving and merciful knowledge."

The discovery of my true self in God is a return to my original identity. It is a reentry into the cosmic dance. It is a recovery of that at-oneness-with-everything in the Hidden Ground of Love.

It is not, as Merton says in *The Asian Journal* (p. 308), that we discover a new unity. We recover an older unity. We have always been one, but we have not always known that we were one. Thus through total awareness I do not become something that I was not; rather I become who I am or, rather, I come at last to know what had been hidden from me for so long: namely, who I am and always have been. Thus Merton in *The Asian Journal*:

> My dear brothers [and sisters],
> we are already one.
> But we imagine that we are not.
> And what we have to recover is our original unity.
> What we have to be is what we are.

9

The Awareness of
Jesus the Christ

"...so that God may be all in all."
(1 Corinthians 15:28)

Awareness of God can be present in different degrees. I have used the word "contemplation" to designate the highest degree of awareness. Such total awareness of God is God's gift to us. The prayer of awareness, which can stand for various levels of awareness (some approaching very close to contemplation — so close at times that they may already be contemplation) disposes us to receive that gift: it is being in the Presence of God apprehended through *faith*. We *believe* that we are in God's Presence. Spending time in the prayer of awareness is letting this faith seep into our depths. Our faith grows and our awareness deepens. This prepares us for the total experience of God's Presence when, in God's own good time, the gift of contemplation is offered us.

Even if this gift is given to us, it never becomes, at least this side of the eternal divide, a permanent possession. Even if we have tasted the sweet joy of total awareness (perfect communion with God, that happiness of being at one with everything, or whatever other descriptive analogy one wants to use) it is an experience that does not remain with us continuously: it comes and goes so that from one moment to the next the degree of our awareness of God's Presence will necessarily vary (though as I have been careful to point out, this does not affect in any way the reality of our *being* in God's Presence — for this is a fact, whether a person is aware of it or not).

Awareness and Christology

There is one person who lived on the face of the earth for whom the prayer of awareness easily and quickly merged into contemplative prayer and for whom such prayer was not a momentary experience, but a fundamental existential reality of his life. This *wholly aware person* was the one whom Christians accept as Lord and Savior: Jesus Christ. He has a humanity like ours — a fact that the New Testament and the early council of the Church go to great lengths to affirm. Arianism, in the fourth century, carried that affirmation so far that it refused to go beyond it to say that Jesus was more than human.

Influence of Arianism

Arianism hit a sensitive nerve in the Christian psyche that brought about a sharp adverse reaction and which led ultimately to a curious development: many Christians were so concerned to say, against the Arians, that Jesus was not *just* human that they ended up by not letting him be truly human at all. This overreaction to Arianism has had a long history and an ongoing influence on the way Christology has been articulated in the Christian West. Traditional Christology has always been carefully orthodox, insisting on the Chalcedon doctrine of the two natures of Christ in the one divine person. There was never any question about the *fact* of his full humanity. The definition of the Council of Chalcedon (A.D. 451) was quite clear: "He is consubstantial with the Father in his divinity, consubstantial with us in his humanity." But, as Christology developed in the Church, the *meaning* of that humanity Jesus shared with us tended to be submerged in his divinity (quite contrary to the definition of Chalcedon) or was so deeply affected by divinity that it was difficult to see that he really was human as we are human. He appeared to be God in a body. He seemed to emerge as a being able to operate in two different fields of action: one human, one divine, as if every time he did anything, he had to decide: what will it be this time? Shall I act as God or as man? This is not the kind of option that comes to mind when we think of being fully human.

The Christology I learned in seminary in the early 1940s (surely a long time after the days of Arius) was still strongly anti-Arian in tone. It was thoroughly orthodox in its expression: it used all the right words. Its great passion (if one may think of such theology as being passionate) was to proclaim the mystery of Jesus Christ clearly and succinctly. It was a theology that manifested the perennial human concern to be as comfortable as possible with mystery by somehow thinking that one had "settled" the mystery by using the correct words. Having done this, one lives amicably with the "untidiness" of mystery by pretending it isn't there. The problem with this way of putting the mind at rest is that we lose the great value that comes from living with mystery. Mystery is not an obstacle to be overcome, but a call to insight: insight that continually clears our thinking, but never exhausts the mystery.

It is so easy for theology to go through three reductionist steps in dealing with mystery. Step one is to articulate the mystery in terms of two truths that seem incompatible with one another. Step two is to affirm both these truths. The third step is to emphasize one of these two truths and simply ignore the other, though without ever denying it.

One of the problems with the Christology I was taught was that, in its explanation of the mystery (like so many Christologies dominated by the anti-Arian strain I spoke of earlier) it progressed through these three steps, finally settling on the third, in which it so staunchly affirmed Jesus' divinity that it was difficult to see much real humanity left in him. Step by step through his life, he knew everything that was going to happen. And if he said that there was something he didn't know (as, for instance, the end of the world), or if he asked a question that seemed to seek information he didn't have (as when the woman in the crowd touched him and was cured and he asked: "Who touched me?"), he was just *pretending* in order to edify us and make us think he really was like us. Or else he was saying: One part of me (the divine) knows this; the other part of me (the human) doesn't. It was as if he had two computer screens before him and knew or didn't, depending on which screen he was looking at. And even his human nature was a very "hyped up" human nature. For instance, this Christology affirmed that Jesus, even from his mother's womb, possessed infused knowledge and the knowledge of the beatific vision: not bad equipment with which to start out the human venture. It was a theological approach that all but justified the quip that, after his birth in Bethlehem, Jesus sat up alert in his crib reading the *New York Times* or, maybe, the *Bethlehem Star*.

Contemporary Biblical Studies and Christology

It has been in the wake of the biblical studies of the past three or four decades that Catholic scholarship has rediscovered the fullness of what it means to say that Jesus is one of us. He was a human being, like us, who suffered pain and heartache, who got hungry and loved to eat and drink, who laughed at times and who also cried. He was a human being moved to compassion toward the poor, the sick, the abused of society and to indignation toward those who did the abusing. He loved his friends and was deeply wounded by the cowardice of some of them when they left him to suffer alone. And he prayed too — sometimes with words (the Epistle to the Hebrews says: "In the days when he was in the flesh, he offered prayers and supplications with loud cries and tears to God" [5:7]); at other times without words (I mentioned in the Introduction the reverent awe with which the disciples watched Jesus as he prayed). Impossible for us to fathom the depths of that deep communion with God that describes the prayer of Jesus.

Jesus' Prayer as a Human Experience

Still when we speak about it, *we have to see Jesus' prayer as a human experience*. Just as the carpenter's son was not an immediate expert in sawing a board correctly or pounding a nail, but had to learn this in the school of experience and under the tutelage of Joseph the master carpenter, so we must understand that his awareness of God was not something that he was born with (much less conceived with) full-blown. Like any other human he grew in this awareness. Being the kind of human being that he was, as his portrait emerges from the pages of the New Testament, that growth must have been spectacular. Some Scripture scholars have tried to see special moments of growth in awareness in particular events in Jesus' life. Thus they would suggest that the baptism of Jesus was the moment that he came to know his own identity as the Messiah of God. Some have gone so far as to say that it was only in his experience of death and resurrection that Jesus came to be aware that he was uniquely the Son of God.

It seems to me that we are ill advised to attempt to "psychologize" the New Testament's portrayal of Jesus. It is difficult to see that this could have been the intent or even the interest of the New Testament writers. Their chief purpose was to present the witness of the preaching and teaching of the early Church to the fact that Jesus was raised by God and "made [by Him] both Lord and Messiah." (The words are Peter's as reported in Acts 2:36.) That the Jesus whom they present was an extraordinary human being is beyond question. His deep compassion, his unconditional love, his complete unselfishness in reaching out to people in all sorts of needs — all these surely suggest one who has acquired the contemplative vision of God and that deep sense of "being at one with everything in that Hidden Ground of Love," whom he dared to call by the endearing name of "Abba." Was the prayer of awareness always in him the prayer of total awareness, so that he was consciously the contemplative from the beginning of his existence? We have no resources to answer such a question. The farthest I would want to go would be to say that, if it was a truly human consciousness of God and all in God, it had to go through some process of growth. What that growth was and how it progressed is part of the fascination of the mystery that is Jesus Christ.

Resurrection and New Life

There is, however, an important point I want to make about Jesus' growth to total consciousness. Whatever we may try to say about the growth and development in self-identity that occurred during his mortal existence, it is surely clear that his "being raised" by God needs to be seen as a decisive and radical transformation of his humanity. It was not that in some miraculous way he *survived* death or *escaped* it. He *experienced* death and went *beyond* it. Death was not able to hold him. His "being raised" put him "on the other side" of death, where there is only life and no mortality. Life that is on the other side of death — the new life Jesus entered upon — is, in ways not even imaginable to us, fundamentally different from human life as we know it.

The new life of the Risen Jesus released him not only from death, but also from those restraints on human existence that are the signs of mortality. Mortal existence forces us to live out our lives in discrete moments at a given time-period and at a particular place. We are prisoners of time and space. But with the Risen One it is different: no longer circumscribed by time and space (as he had been in his mortal existence), he has become and forever remains the contemporary of every age and the Savior-in-residence of every place.

Try to imagine what this means in terms of the theme of this book: awareness of God and a deep consciousness of all persons, of all created reality, in God. The Risen Jesus' sense of being-at-one with all that is was the experience of total communion with all reality, not in some general sort of way, but with everything in its own unique singularity. To put this very concretely it was and is a profound consciousness of communion with each and every person who lived from the beginning of time till now. Just to say this is to say the incomprehensible. When I say it, I have to admit quite literally that I don't know what I am talking about. The words blow my mind — quite literally. They empty it of all thoughts and concepts. In fact they leave me with meaning I can find only in God. One might even react by saying that what I am really affirming is that in the resurrection of Jesus he became God. And actually that isn't too far from the way the first Christians saw the significance of the raising of Jesus: the One who had lived among them had *become* God. This was the kind of language Peter used in his sermon on the first Christian Pentecost, wherein he tells the people: "This Jesus whom you crucified God has made to be both Lord and Messiah." In understanding this passage, one needs to know that the word for "Lord" here is the Greek word *"Kurios,"* which is the Greek translation of the Holy Name of God (YHWH).

Somehow this seemed at the time to be the easiest way of putting it. They had known this man who had lived among them. Now that they see the transformation that has been accomplished in him, the seemingly logical statement is that this human being became God. But it is a logic that is demolished by even a momentary reflection on the Reality that God actually is. One does not *become* God. God simply is. Inexplicable though it is, we find ourselves needing to say not that Jesus of Nazareth became God, but that he is God. It falls too short of the reality to say that in him humanity became God; rather we have to say God became humanity. Or to use the words of the Fourth Gospel: "The Word became flesh and made his dwelling among us." The culmination of Jesus' human awareness is the awareness that he is God's Son in so unique a sense that we can say that he is God.

This takes us back to Bethlehem. Was Jesus in a manger very God? A "no" answer would straightway plunge us into heresy; a "yes" answer into the profoundest mystery. Our tongues are tied in speaking about him. Yet not really; for, whatever it means to say he is divine, it still remains — as defined Christian truth — that he is fully human and we can therefore talk about him in that way — as largely we have been doing in this chapter. We see accomplished in him a level of awareness that is human, yet takes his humanity beyond its humanness into God.

To put this in the language of the New Testament, Jesus is the One in whom God's reign has come — fully and totally. In his life and death and new Life God's love totally rules. In Jesus oneness with God is so fully achieved that he is named in the New Testament the "Son of God." All those things that contradict God's reign — sin, selfishness, divisiveness, destructiveness, alienation — are dealt with and radically overcome in his life and especially in his death and his "being raised." The cross of Christ symbolizes his death and at the same time God's putting the seal of approval on Jesus by raising him from the dead. The tree in the garden that in the myth of the fall brought sin and alienation into the world, disrupting its harmony and oneness, finds its reversal in the tree of Jesus' cross, which brings everlasting life and true at-one-ment into the world once again. The grace of God that will ultimately achieve the full triumph of God's reign is already radically present in the world in Jesus, the Christ, the Son of God. The way back to paradise is revealed. The discovery — or, perhaps better, the *recovery* — of that oneness with God in harmony with all reality, hidden (as it has been) by human alienation, has become a true human possibility offered to us through the risen Jesus. Contemplative awareness, with all that it implies, is now placed within the human grasp.

New Life Shared: Salvation through Christ

The heart of the New Testament teaching is that Jesus Christ is not only the exemplar of the new humanity (i.e., the one who "made it" himself and offers a model for our imitation); he is likewise for us the cause of that new humanity (he makes it happen in us). Having his humanity taken into God in his "being-raised," he was empowered to take the rest of humanity into God with him. In Pauline language he was "the first-born of many brothers [and sisters]" (Rom. 8:29). The Scripture reading for the feast of Christmas (from the second chapter of the Epistle to Titus) puts it quite simply: "The grace of God has appeared offering salvation to all peoples." And it is offered in and through Christ. He proffers the invitation; he also leads us to the "place" to which we are invited. He not only guides us; he "carries" us, as the shepherd carries the sheep on his shoulders. Or, to put the theme of salvation in terms of the theme of this book: he brings us to awareness of God: he leads us from unawareness, through various degrees of awareness, to its final stage which is everlasting contemplation.

Awareness as the "Cosmic Dance"

In the previous chapter I mentioned how Merton compared the "original state" before the fall to the cosmic dance: the whole universe moving in harmonious rhythm with God. One way of describing salvation is to say that Jesus the Christ not only recovers the harmony of that dance in himself; he leads us and the whole universe in the cosmic dance. The metaphor is a fruitful one for reflecting on our salvation in Christ.

In writing about the cosmic dance in the final chapter of *New Seeds of Contemplation* Merton is quite consciously making use of an ancient English carol, "Tomorrow is my dancing day," which he describes, in a letter to Edward Deming Andrews, as "a lovely carol about the dancing of God with man in the mystery of the Incarnation" (see *The Hidden Ground of Love*, p. 34). The carol is made up of eleven stanzas, to each of which the following refrain is added:

> Sing, O my love, O my love,
> my love, my love.
> This have I done for my true love.

The first two stanzas are about Christmas and the Incarnation. The first says:

> Tomorrow shall be my dancing day,
> I would my true love did so chance
> to see the legend of my play,
> to call my true love to the dance.

This phrase "to call my true love to the dance," or a variation of it, is repeated at the end of each stanza, prior to the refrain inviting the true love to sing. Hence each stanza concludes with an invitation to dance and sing.

The second stanza is also about the Incarnation and the notion of the dance begins to take on wider dimensions of solidarity with the whole human race. And the purpose of that solidarity (there is the lovely image of being "knit" to human nature) was for salvation — that he might lead us in his dance: the dance of harmony and unity, the dance of contemplation. Notice that it is my "true love" who is being called to the dance. "True love" is a singular noun that turns out, meaningwise, to be plural: it stands for all of God's people, indeed for all of creation; for all that God made is the object of God's love and is called to the dance.

> Then was I born of a virgin pure,
> of her I took fleshly substance;
> Thus was I knit to man's nature
> To call my true love to my dance.

Stanza four speaks of Jesus' baptism, in which the Holy Ghost did on him glance and his Father's voice was heard calling "my true love to *my* dance." At this point in the carol the dance is Jesus' dance and it is to that dance that God calls his people. God wills to save through Jesus. It is the dance led by Jesus that brings us back to harmony and oneness with God.

The fifth stanza and the sixth speak of the dark side of Jesus' life: temptation, enmity, betrayal. The devil does his best to persuade Jesus to give up the leading of the dance.

> The devil bade me make stones my bread,
> To have me break my true love's dance.

And there is the darkness of betrayal by one of his own. Judas is the symbol of a weak and sometimes perverse humanity continually threatening to destroy the rhythm of the dance. When he sold Jesus, Judas, "his covetousness for to advance," tells the guards with him:

> Mark whom I kiss, the same do hold
> The same is he shall lead the dance.

Significantly the mark that Judas gives to his companions to identify Jesus is that he is the one who is *the leader of the dance*. The
forces of darkness that create alienation and disharmony cannot
bide the presence of one who brings unity and communion. They
must seize him and eventually destroy him. Thus, there is the
seeming defeat that comes with death. "They scourged me and
set me at nought/Judging me to die to lead the dance." This
verse intrigues because it could be read to mean he was put to
death either (1) for wanting to lead the dance or (2) in order that
he might lead it. If the latter meaning is taken, the stanza embodies a doctrine of atonement: it was Jesus' death that restored the
harmony of creation. His death accomplishes our "at-one-ment"
with God.

Stanza nine speaks of his crucifixion and suggests a theme
dear to very early Christian tradition, namely, that the Church,
the community of those whom Jesus makes one with God,
was born from his pierced side. The water and blood that is-
sued from his side symbolized baptism and the Eucharist, the
two great sacraments that create the Church and enable us
to appropriate Christ's victory and in him become one with
God.

> Then on the cross hanged I was,
> where a spear to my heart did glance;
> There issued forth both water and blood
> To call my true love to the dance.

This striking carol concludes, in stanzas ten and eleven, with
the victory of Jesus — a victory described in terms of the dance.

> Then down to hell I took my way
> For my true love's deliverance.
> And rose again on the third day
> Up to my true love and the dance.
>
> Then up to heaven I did ascend,
> Where now I dwell in sure substance
> On the right hand of God that man
> May come unto the general dance.

Probably someone is going to say (if he or she has not said it already) that I am squeezing more out of this carol than I ought; yet I want to ask such a long-suffering reader to indulge me in just a bit more such "squeezing." For I want to suggest that a subtle change takes place in the final verse. It speaks of Jesus' return to God and then, suddenly and abruptly, the dance that all through the carol has been Jesus' dance becomes the "general dance." Is there any significance in this change? Does this adjective offer some new meaning?

I want to approach this question by discussing briefly a critique (not necessarily a criticism) that some people have made about some of the things I have said and written about spirituality. I have been told that the spirituality I speak and write about is *God-centered*, rather than *Christ-centered*. In response I would say that this evaluation of the approach to spirituality that I try to present is correct: it is a God-centered spirituality. To me it seems that this is the way all spirituality must be. To speak of a *Christ-centered spirituality* is surely not incorrect, but it is a penultimate way of expressing the meaning of spirituality. It is describing spirituality as a *way* rather than as a *goal*. Jesus is God's person and ours: he leads us to God. He brings us back to the primitive awareness of God that was our "original face before we were born." Jesus, for the Christian at least, is essential to our spirituality; but it is God who is ultimate. That is why I find it interesting that, in the carol we have been reflecting on, Jesus' dance becomes in the last stanza the "general dance." It becomes, I would want to say, God's dance. Shorn of metaphor, it means that Jesus makes possible for us that full awareness of God's Presence that we call contemplation and that is the final goal of all human existence: the experienced oneness with God that comes with this total consciousness of God. Jesus the Christ, the paradigm of the new humanity, brings us back to God our Father/Mother. This it seems to me is what Paul is saying in that majestic passage in the fifteenth chapter of 1 Corinthians, in which — speaking in cosmic terms — he tells us that in the end God will subject all things, including finally even death, to Christ. Then Paul orchestrates to a soaring climax:

When, finally, all has been subjected to the Son,
he will then subject himself
to the One who made all things subject to him,
so that *God may be all in all*. (1 Cor. 15:28)

A FOOTNOTE TO CHAPTER NINE:
PRESENCE, REAL PRESENCE,
EUCHARISTIC PRESENCE

Real Presence, Eucharistic Presence

Throughout this book I have been using the word "Presence" to refer to God, not simply as a Being among other beings, but as "the Hidden Ground of Love" in which each and every created being finds its identity, its uniqueness, its interrelatedness. All created reality exists in God; apart from God there is nothing. And when I speak of all created beings, I mean to include the humanity of Christ. For if it is true humanity (and to deny this would be heresy), it must be created.

Yet, as I have already made clear (hopefully), a transformation of Christ's humanity took place when God raised him from the dead. His humanity's existence broke the barriers of space and time and gave him, in his very humanness, something of the ubiquity that belongs to God. He is really present in the world, not in mortal fashion, but spiritually. When I say, "spiritually," though, I want to make clear that I am not opposing it to "really": it is the whole Christ who is present. He is present through his Spirit. There are times when we say of a valiant person who has died: "his spirit lives on," by which we mean that the memory of his valiant deeds survives his departure from our midst. The memory of what he did continues even after he has left us in death. This is *not* what we mean when we say that Jesus is present among us through his Spirit. His Spirit, who is the very Spirit of God (and indeed, properly understood, our Spirit too) makes his whole self, in the fullness of his glorified humanity, truly present among us. He is among us in a dynamic way, acting in our midst to incorporate us into himself, gathering us into one that we might recover that awareness of God that was his so dazzlingly on earth and now in so incomprehensible a way in his Risen Life. Awakening us to oneness and to all the responsibilities that this oneness calls us to, he is present to mature our consciences and rouse them to action on behalf of our needy sisters and brothers. He is there to deepen our respect for all created things. He is there to give us glimpses of the cosmic dance. Finally, having made us one with himself, he will be able to hand us over to God. Thus, as Paul said: "God will be all in all." This is the fundamental *Real Presence* of Jesus in our midst. Any other way of speaking of his Presence must always be understood in terms of this widest understanding of that Presence as a Presence that flows from the very fact of new Risen Life.

Eucharistic Presence

For many people the term "Real Presence" of Jesus Christ means simply and solely his sacramental presence in the Eucharist. One of the many beneficent results of the Second Vatican Council is that it has considerably expanded our understanding of the term "Real Presence." In the Constitution on the Liturgy and in subsequent documents on liturgy, four kinds of presence were distinguished: (1) Jesus' presence in the community that gathers in his name for worship; (2) his presence in the Word of Scripture, as God's Word is proclaimed in liturgy; (3) his presence in the priest-minister who acts in his name; and (4) his presence in the sacrament in the bread and wine that becomes the food that feeds and deepens our communion with God and with one another.

We need to reflect, if only briefly, on these ways in which Christ is present in the Eucharist. I recall one time when, being distracted while distributing the Holy Bread at Communion, I inadvertently changed the accompanying words. Instead of *"This* is the Body of Christ," which I was supposed to say, I suddenly heard myself saying: "You are the Body of Christ." A felicitous mistake putting unexpected words on a whole new dimension of the Eucharistic gathering, namely, the Real Presence of Christ in the assembled community of faith. Word-Presence is also a form of *real* Presence. Think of being in a room with another person where each of you is reading in a different corner of the room. Then, on a sudden impulse, you desire to share what you have been reading with the other. Conversation ensues. Your presence to one another is changed. It is no longer physical presence merely, it is a typically human way of being present — through dialogue and conversation. Christ is also present, the council says, in the person of the priest-minister who presides at the Eucharist. The words that the priest speaks in the Eucharistic Prayer do indeed indicate Christ acting in and through him, though I would want to wonder at least if this is not a particular specification of the first way of Presence in the Eucharist: Christ's Presence in the assembled people, including the one who presides. Finally, there is in the Eucharist that most excellent form of Presence: Jesus' Presence in the sacramental species.

True Eucharistic renewal demands not only that we expand our understanding of what Real Presence is, but also that we deepen our realization of what it means. *Jesus is not present in the Eucharist in order that we may adore him* (as a spirituality of devotion tends to emphasize) but *in order that he may transform us into himself by drawing us into the mystery of his death and resurrection.* His Presence is not a static presence (just being there); it is a dynamic Presence: He is there to re-create us into his own image. That is why in the Eucharistic prayer there are two *epicleses.* (*Epiclesis* is a Greek word that means "the invocation of the Holy Spirit.") The first *epiclesis* is the consecratory one, in which the Spirit is called upon to transform the bread and wine into the Body and Blood of Christ. Thus in the second Eucharistic prayer of the Roman Sacramentary the priest prays: "Let your Spirit come upon these gifts to make them holy, so that they may become the Body and Blood of our Lord Jesus Christ." But there is a second *epiclesis* that calls upon God to send the Holy Spirit to transform us, his people, into the Body of Christ. In the first of the Eucharistic Prayers for Reconciliation, for instance, the priest prays: "Father, look with love on those you have called to share in the one sacrifice of Christ. By the power of your Holy Spirit make them one Body healed of all division."

The second *epiclesis* demands more of the Holy Spirit than the first. The bread is inert and readily yields itself to be transformed into Christ. It is with much greater difficulty that we give up our petty selves to be transformed into the Body of Christ. Yet the first transformation (of the bread into the Body of Christ) has meaning only insofar as it symbolizes and brings about the transformation of God's people into the Body of Christ.

An older Roman Catholic theology laid great stress on the obligation of the Sunday Eucharist. There is a "Sunday obligation," but it is not simply the "obligation of being there." This obligation means, in the first place, our duty to praise and thank God on the Lord's Day. But it also means a duty of concern and compassion for people, our oneness with those with whom we celebrate in the Eucharist. As William J. Byron has written: "To sit in solitude in a pew without concern for or interest in the community gathered there leaves much of the Sunday obligation unfulfilled." The Eucharist ought to serve as

> a magnet to draw people out of their private hiding places, to help them break down the barriers of egoism and petty self-interest, to overcome the artificial and often destructive divisions of social and economic class, of race, [of sex,] and even of age." (William J. Byron, "Eucharist and Society," *America*, August 7, 1976)

From the beginning of their existence Christian people have gathered on the first day of the week to remember Jesus and by the remembering to celebrate the reality of his Presence and Action in the midst of the community. This gathering is the Sunday Eucharist.

Sometimes, in moments of bereavement following the death of a loved one, a person may suddenly and inexplicably experience the "presence" of the deceased. Though it may be a vivid and moving moment, it is brief and quickly over. This was the way in which the earliest Christians experienced Jesus. Their awareness of Jesus was not like the sense of suddenly "feeling" the presence of a deceased loved one that may come to a person in moments of bereavement. Thomas Merton, you will perhaps remember, had such an experience of his father in a hotel room in Rome. He wrote about it in *The Seven Storey Mountain:* "Suddenly it seemed to me that Father, who had now been dead more than a year, was there with me. The sense of his presence was as vivid and as real and as startling as if he had touched my arm or spoken to me. The whole thing passed in a flash."

This was not the way the early Christians experienced the Risen Jesus. In the words of Angela Tilby: "St. Paul, in his earliest epistles, written probably about twenty years after the death of Jesus, writes of Christ as a kind of divine atmosphere. Those who believe are "in Christ." Just as believers in God feel surrounded by a "Presence," so the first Christians seem to be aware of Christ surrounding and supporting them" (p. 71).

10

Church: Community of Those Who Are Aware

"We are Easter people and 'alleluia' is our song."
(St. Augustine)

Jesus is the model of total awareness of God. Mystery that we can only marvel at, his was an awareness that was always there. It was not only a full consciousness of God, but of all reality in God. More deeply than any of us he experienced the meaning of our oneness with one another.

Death for Jesus, therefore, was not — as it is for most of us — a transition into total awareness of God. He already had that total awareness. What death and resurrection meant for him was that he entered into a new kind of life, an immortal life, in which it became clear that the fullness of the deity existed in him. So profound was his awareness of God that he (as any sort of separate entity) simply was not there. Only God was there.

The First-Born of Many Sisters and Brothers
In this completely new existence Jesus the Christ became God's instrument in enabling all of us eventually to attain to this full awareness. This is what Paul means when he speaks of Jesus as the "first-born of many sisters and brothers," and when he describes Christ as the head of the Church and the Church as his Body. He is talking about that oneness of all created reality with God and how it is through the grace of God, freely given in Christ, that we attain to awareness of this oneness. It is "in Christ" that we are able to overcome the dualities of life that prevent us from experiencing our oneness with God, with one another and with the whole world. This phrase "to be in Christ" is a rich phrase in

the theology of St. Paul. It is what he means by being a person: we are persons not in isolation, but in oneness with one another. This phrase "to be in Christ" is also a way in which Paul describes the Church as the "Body of Christ." In chapter 12 of 1 Corinthians Paul develops at great length the analogy of the body to portray the Church:

> The body is one and has many members,
> but all the members, many though they are, are one body;
> and so it is with Christ....
> You, then, are the body of Christ.
> Every one of you is a member of it. (1 Cor. 12:12, 25)

And in chapter 15 — a text I have already mentioned — Paul indicates how at the end all will be subject to Christ, and Christ in turn will hand everything over to God so that God may be "all in all."

A Description of Church

One way of describing the Church, therefore, is to say that it is the communion of men and women who are aware (in varying degrees of depth) of their oneness with God in Christ. To be "totally aware of God" is to realize the full potential of "being in Christ," and, therefore of being Church.

Married couples who deeply love one another enjoy going out on occasion to celebrate. It may be an anniversary or a birthday or even St. Valentine's day. Such celebrations are occasions that bring back happy memories: perhaps the first date they had, or the day they were engaged, or the day they were married. And, if you want to get really sentimental, even schmaltzy about it, perhaps they ask the band or orchestra to play "their song," that is, a song associated with some special moment of tenderness and growth in their relationship. Hearing it would bring that moment back to their minds and renew the thrill of that precious moment of the past. Their celebrating brings them to a new degree of awareness of their oneness with one another.

I want to speak in this chapter about the reality that we call "Church," first of all, because I would not want anyone to get the idea that the spirituality I am proposing — centering around awareness of the Presence of God — is in any way a privatized spirituality. Quite the contrary. An urgent sense of responsibility for my sisters and brothers is the inevitable offspring of this spirituality. But, second, I want to talk about Church because I am convinced that all too many people, through no fault of their own, tend to believe that "Church" designates a reality that is impersonal, remote, outside them, and not very much involved in their daily life. Third, I feel the need to emphasize that the real life of the Church is to be located, not in institutional structures (necessary though these are), but in the lived experience of God's people moving toward greater consciousness of their own identity in Christ and their oneness with one another.

For those who understand what Church really is, thinking and speaking about "Church" may touch deep chords in their hearts. The word may well evoke sentiments similar to those that I have suggested a couple might associate with an anniversary or a Valentine's Day celebration or even with the playing of their "special song." For the Church is first and foremost not something outside us, but has to do with a unique relationship of communion with God that we have as a people: a relationship that, if properly understood, is a love-relationship quite capable of evoking sentiments of love and endearment, such as any couple in love might experience in a special celebration of their love or in the hearing of "their song."

St. Augustine expressed this very well centuries ago when he described the Christian community in these words: "We are Easter people and 'alleluia' is our song." It is the Easter experience, first of Jesus and then of ourselves in him, that makes us the people, the kind of lovers, we are. And it is in the Easter experience that we hear "our song." "Alleluia" is our song, and every time we hear it we can say, to the Lord Jesus and to one another, what a loving couple might say to each other: "They are playing our song."

So central is the Easter experience for us and so appropriate is "alleluia" as our song that during the Lenten season, as we prepare for a renewed experience of the Easter reality, we give up *our song* for those forty days. Indeed, in some monasteries, on the day before Ash Wednesday — the day that the last "alleluia" will be sung until the Easter Vigil Eucharist — they have a ceremony in which they "bury" the "alleluia" somewhere, only to raise it from its burial place on Easter.

This giving up of the "alleluia," of "our song," for this brief time each year is a kind of dramatic symbol that, because of our sinfulness and selfishness and neglect, part of us has died and we have to go through a period of reconciliation, amendment, and renewal so that on Easter that part of us which was dead may come back to life again. And in that coming back to life again, we become more deeply aware of our communion with one another in Christ and, therefore, are more fully "Easter people," feeling once again free to sing "our song": Alleluia. Lent is a time of recovering and discovering anew our identity as "Easter people" and experiencing more fully what it means to live in conscious awareness of our oneness with God and with each other.

I would like to develop, further, what I mean when I say we are "Easter people." I want to make it clear that this is not just one title that may be given to us, as if there are others: as if, for instance, it could be said that we are "Advent people" and "Christmas people" and "Epiphany people." No, all these terms express realities that unite us to Jesus, but the term that embraces them all is "Easter." Apart from Easter, none of the other names that might be used of us has any meaning. It is "Easter," and Easter alone, that gives ultimate meaning to the whole Christian reality. If we try to talk about ourselves apart from our Easter experience, we are not talking about who we really are.

What I want to insist upon is that, reduced to its least common denominator, the Church is nothing more or less than a community of men and women who witness, in their persons, in their thinking, in their values, indeed in the whole of their lives, to the resurrection of Jesus and to all that that implies for him and for us.

The Resurrection creates the Church. For it means Jesus the Christ is at the right hand of God and is, therefore, able to send the Spirit of God upon us. We are able to receive this Spirit of God and able to begin to enter, in part at least, into the new life that Jesus has already entered into fully. We enter into Jesus' awareness of God. One day all that will remain of us is what is of God and we shall experience fully that we are in God. As for the present, the resurrection of Jesus places us as his followers in a whole new relationship of oneness with God or, better, a new awareness of a oneness that always has been. We now consciously share his life, even though as yet only at a beginning stage, as it were. Our consciousness has a long way to grow. St. John says to us: "We are already God's children. What we shall be has not yet appeared." That is one of those "wow" statements in the New Testament. It's like telling a caterpillar: "You're going to be a butterfly." The reality of being a butterfly is far beyond the comprehension of a caterpillar. It can't possibly imagine what it will mean to be a butterfly. But eventually it will take place and that creature of God will enter into a new and hitherto unsuspected kind of existence. Something similar is our experience that we are God's children now (we already live with some kind of awareness of God's Presence), but what that will mean in its fullness, we simply cannot comprehend. St. John says to us, equivalently: "You haven't seen anything yet!"

Even though we cannot know the fullness of what it means to enter into Jesus' risen life, there are yet two questions we have to deal with, using whatever knowledge we are able to possess. The first question is: what does it mean *to be* "Easter people"? And the second is: what does it mean *to live* as "Easter people"? Though we may never be able to plumb their depths, these are the two fundamental questions that the followers of Jesus have had to grapple with ever since the moment they heard the message and came to believe it, namely: "He is risen. He goes before you."

Faith, Morality, Spirituality

The reflection of the Christian community on what it means to *be* an Easter people is what we have come to formulate into what we call doctrines. The reflection of the Christian community on what it means to *live* as Easter people is what we have come to formulate into what we call "morals" or "Christian morality," and, as the underpinnings and an animating spirit of that morality, Christian spirituality.

The doctrines of the Church constitute an ever-growing body of truths about the risen Lord Jesus, about God, about the Church, about us its members, about the sacraments. As we have reflected on these matters of faith, we have added to them. Sometimes what we have added has enriched our understanding. There have been times, however, in the Church's history when our understanding of faith got hardened into formulas that seemed to have little connection with the experience we were having as Christians. One of the reasons that Jesus sent the Holy Spirit upon his followers was in order that he might lead us out of such periods of dryness: periods when what we said we believed seemed to have little or no relevance to the kind of lives we were living.

But besides the doctrines that come out of the reflections about what and who we believe we are, there are also reflections that come out of the way we live the Christian faith. In our efforts to live the call and challenge of the Gospel, certain ways of acting emerge that clearly appear to be in conflict with the Gospel and other modes of action that seem to be responsible ways of responding to the call of the Gospel. In some cases it would be relatively easy to see what courses of action accorded with the Gospel and what did not. Other situations might not be so clear; and there are times when we have to live with questions and search for satisfactory answers. Yet to do so is much better than accepting inadequate answers, simply because we feel uncomfortable living with questions and insist on having an answer now, no matter what. Sometimes this need to have an immediate answer at all costs has meant a sacrifice of true integrity in our fidelity to the Gospel and to Jesus Christ.

Gifts to the Church: The New Testament

As the Christian community started its journey through history, were there any special gifts of God that would help that community in its reflection on what it believed and how it ought to act so that it could remain faithful to its identity as "Easter people" whose song was "alleluia"? Yes, and we might mention two special gifts. The first was the New Testament Scriptures that gradually came into existence, as the preaching and teaching of the earliest witnesses were put into writing: those witnesses who had known the Lord Jesus in his earthly sojourn and were witnesses of his appearances in his risen life. The Scriptures thus became a kind of norm — against which Christian people could measure their understanding of what it meant to be "Easter people" committed in love and loyalty to the Risen Jesus.

Gift of Leadership

The other special gift I want to mention was a group of leaders who, under the guidance of the Holy Spirit, came to be chosen from the community: not of course in order to lord it over the rest of the community (this Jesus had explicitly forbidden to any one who would be a leader among his disciples) but to exercise an authority of service. They were to lead the community by serving them.

One of the ways in which authority in the Church was able to serve the whole community was by taking the reflections that grew out of the experience of the Christian community and formulating those experiences in the form of doctrines and also moral rules and commitments that could be helpful to the community in understanding what it meant to be "Easter people." Obviously, such formulations had their limitations. For no amount of words could spell out in their fullness and in the concreteness of daily life all that it meant to be "Easter people." But the formulations did at least offer guidelines that were helpful in striving to grasp the challenge to daily living of the Gospel.

From the very beginning the Church believed that this evolving authority in the Church (and it did go through an extensive kind of growth, especially in the beginning) was a way in which the Holy Spirit used some of the members of the community to help preserve the whole community in the truth of the Gospel. The Church was very careful, though, to guard against a kind of Gnosticism that would seem to suggest that authority in the Church had access to the truth in a way that was closed to the rest of the members of the community. It was clearly understood that the Spirit operated in the whole Church: among the whole people, women and men. Hence those who were to express the teachings of the Church — whether in matters of faith, morals, or spirituality — obviously needed to consult the experience of the whole Church.

Historical Context

This community of Easter people, whose song was "alleluia," does not live out its life and its commitments to the Gospel in a vacuum, but in the context of history. That means that inevitably the culture, the times, the attitudes of people at a particular moment of history would influence the ways in which the community comes to express the faith it professed, the moral stances it adopts, and the spiritual life it strives to live.

The fundamental problem that the Christian community has had to face in any given age is how to bring together the heritage of the past and make it relevant to the needs of the present.

Perhaps no Church document has expressed such acute awareness of this problem as the document on the Church in the modern world (*Gaudium et Spes*) of Vatican II. Stating that the Church's only goal is "to carry forward the work of Christ himself under the lead of the befriending Spirit," this document goes on to say:

> To carry out such a task the Church has always had the duty of scrutinizing the signs of the times and of interpreting them in the light of the Gospel. Thus, in language intelligible to each generation, she can respond to the perennial questions which people ask about this present life and the life to come, and about the relationship of the one to the other. We must therefore recognize and understand the world in which we live, its expectations, its longings, and its often dramatic characteristics. (Art.4)

What this document is saying to us is that *we have to learn in our own time, our own history, our own culture what it means to be "Easter people" whose song is "alleluia."* Nor are we to think that the search for authentic human living is an enterprise that only the Christian community is engaged in. Thus this same document tells us:

> In fidelity to conscience, Christians are joined with the rest of human beings in the search for truth, and for the genuine solution to the numerous problems which arise in the lives of individuals and from social relationships. (Art. 16)

Competence of Laypersons in the Church

The Council Fathers of Vatican II also gave clear signals that this task of coming to know what it means to be "Easter people" in our day should not be thought of as a task simply for the hierarchy and the clergy of the Church. It is the affair of all God's people. Thus we read in article 42 of this same document about the distinctive role that the laity must play in the life of the Church. We are told:

> Let the layperson not imagine that their pastors are always such experts, that to every problem which arises, however complicated, they can readily give him a concrete solution, or even that such is their mission. Rather, enlightened by Christian wisdom and giving close attention to the teaching authority of the Church, let the layperson take on his or her distinctive role.

Realizing that there will be legitimate differences of opinion among the faithful on a given matter, we are admonished "to enlighten one another through honest discussion, preserving mutual charity and caring above all for the common good." In article 62 of this document, the importance of freedom of inquiry in the Church is clearly expressed. Thus we are told:

> Let it be recognized that all the faithful, clerical and lay, possess a lawful freedom of inquiry and of thought, and the freedom to express their minds humbly and courageously about those matters in which they enjoy competence.

What the Second Vatican Council said, loud and clear, is that we are all involved in this process of coming to know ever more deeply, though never fully, what it means to be "Easter people" whose song is "alleluia." There is a teaching authority in the Church charged with the responsibility of guiding us in this enterprise. But we must insist: it is not their enterprise alone that the rest of us watch from the sidelines; it is a task that falls to all of us. None of us can abdicate his or her part of that responsibility. For recognizing this responsibility is part of our awareness of our own identity and our oneness in Christ with all God's people.

It seems to me that one of the areas where the laity have abdicated their responsibility (or, probably a better way of putting it, have never really been allowed to exercise it) is the area of sexuality, especially as that pertains to married people. A recent editorial in the *London Tablet* offered the suggestion that the Church — by which I am sure the editor meant the hierarchical and clerical Church) ought to accept a self-imposed moratorium of not making any statements about human sexuality for the next fifty years. In the light of some of the statements that have emerged in recent times on this subject, this proposal strikes me as one well worth considering. Such a self-imposed silence on the part of Church authority might lead to reflections on what human sexuality means to "Easter people" that would come from married people, from people who are not vowed to a life of celibacy. The Second Vatican Council said that people who have competence in a particular area ought to speak out in that area for the good of the whole Church. Yet it would seem that for centuries in the Roman Catholic Church statements about sexuality have been forthcoming from those people in the Church who could be presumed to possess the most limited knowledge of the experience of human sexuality.

Once again, let me make the point that we must not subscribe to a Gnostic position that would hold that the teaching authority of the Church has some kind of special access to truth that is not open to other members of the Christian community. If they are to teach authentically, they must be in touch with what God's "Easter people" are experiencing as they seek to live out the call and challenge of the Gospel in their own life situations.

A Time of Tension

We live at a time of uneasiness in the Church. It is a time when authority in the Church seems to feel itself beleaguered, almost as if theologians and people were fighting it. It would be better to say they are fighting to be heard at a time when authority all too often ignores dialogue and seeks to impose its positions (carved out of a particular theological perspective) on the whole Church. We have to work for a return of harmony in the Church. Yet we have to keep our priorities straight. The Church is God's people seeking God's will and striving to deepen their sense of awareness of our oneness with God and with one another. It is only in and through this kind of awareness that the Church is able to be what it is intended to be and is able to accomplish what it exists to accomplish: namely, to participate in the work of the Lord Jesus in handing over all to God, so that God may be All in all.

Some of the things I have been trying to express about Church come out of my reading of the writings of an extraordinary person: a Catholic layman who was an authority on theology and mysticism at a time when lay folk were not expected to be authorities in either of these fields. Baron Friedrich von Hügel, a devout Catholic born in the mid-nineteenth century, who relished writing long letters (filled with learned intuitions and spiritual counsel) to a favorite niece, and who was involved in the Modernist crisis of the early twentieth century (which crisis left him neither condemned nor unscathed), often reflected in his books and letters on the realities that make up the Church. In *The Mystical Elements of Religion*, he makes the point that in all religions there are three elements: the institutional, the intellectual, and the mystical. He believed the Church was at its best when harmony existed among these three.

By the *mystical* element of the Church, he means to designate the people of the Church, the community of the faithful. Earlier in this book (and also in *Seeking the Face of God*, I have tried to make clear that at the deepest level of our being, we are all "contemplatives" ("mystics"). Hence von Hügel's position that the faithful constitute the "mystical" element of the Church is most congenial to the theme of this book. Yet I would dare say that many people in the Church (maybe most?) would find it quite puzzling to have themselves cast in such a role in the Church. They certainly have not been brought up to think of themselves as "mystical." Yet what von Hügel means by this, it seems clear to me, is that God is present among people and, whether they are aware of it or not, God is acting continually among them to save them: sustaining them in existence, uniting them to one another at the deepest possible level, and challenging them to responsibility. Some people are aware, in varying degrees, of this divine Presence and because of this awareness can be called "mystics" (or "contemplatives," to use the term we have been using throughout this book). Others might be called "masked contemplatives" (to use a term that Merton used in some of his earlier writings): they are indeed in the Presence of God (and therefore there is this contemplative ["mystical"] element in their lives); yet they are not yet aware of that Presence.

It should be clear that the other two elements in the Church (the "intellectual" and the "institutional") exist to foster the "mystical" life of the Church. For the very *raison d'être* of the Church is to enable all people to find themselves in God and in the finding discover their sisters and brothers and the responsibilities we all have for one another. In fact, those who comprise the "intellectual" and "institutional" elements of the Church are not separate from the people of God. For they are first members of the community of faith, before they assume the particular responsibilities that belong to their specialized status in the Church. (Indeed, I might make the point that this tendency to separate the "professionals" [clergy and theologians, but especially clergy] from the laity within the community of faith is another indication of what I have earlier called "spiritual apartheid.")

By the *intellectual* element of the Church, von Hügel means to refer, as one could easily guess, to the theologians whose specific task on behalf of all the faithful is to articulate as clearly as possible an understanding of the faith, the morality, and the spirituality by which the community lives.

Theologians do not always agree on the way in which the faith of the Christian community should be expressed. Such diversity can be a sign of enrichment for the people of God. At times, however, it can become a cause of perplexity and bewilderment. Clearly the Church is not intended to be an endless debating society, in which nothing is definitive. It is for this reason that there must be this third, or *institutional*, element in the Church. There must be something or someone in the Church with the divinely given authority to gather up the experience going on in the community of faith, and all this thinking that theologians have put in writing, and finally make a judgment that would put the community's seal of authenticity on what is truly the faith of the Church. The role of making this judgment — and for Roman Catholics this was divinely ordained — fell to a group who very early in the Church's history came to be known as bishops and whose collegial task, in union with their head, the bishop of Rome, was to say with some finality: "This is our faith. This we believe."

Yet such judgments must never be arbitrary. They must grow out of the lived experience of the Church. This requires that if the *"institutional* element" is to make its proper contribution to the harmony of the Church's life, it must keep in close touch with the experience that is going on in the community of the faithful and with the reflection that is being articulated by the theologians of the Church. For the teachings of the Church do not, like the Emerald Isle, "fall from out the sky one day." The Christian people's understanding of what God is doing among them offers the "raw material" out of which such teachings should emerge. It is a matter of Catholic faith that, when certain conditions are fulfilled, the college of bishops under the headship of the pope is infallible. The charism of infallibility is a guarantee that the Church's teachings will be protected from *error*. It is no guarantee, however, that they will be protected from *irrelevance*, especially if they are put forth without serious consideration of the religious experiences of the faithful.

The Local Church

That oneness with God, the Hidden Ground of Love in all of reality — a oneness that the Church exists to discover — is not a kind of amorphous conglomerate of unity: it exists in precise ways at various levels. One level that is most important for us to consider is the unity at the level of the local church. It is especially in the local church that we experience ourselves as "Easter people."

A story about a World War I chaplain, Fr. Francis Patrick Duffy, will clarify what I mean. Fr. Duffy is well known as the chaplain of the Fighting 69th Division. (There is a statue in his honor between 46th and 47th Streets in Duffy Square, New York City). One day on the battlefield a soldier approached him. The soldier knew that he was a chaplain, but did not know the Church he belonged to. So he asked: "Are you a *Roman* Catholic?" Fr. Duffy paused for a moment and then answered: "Well, actually, I'm a *New York* Catholic."

His answer embodied an excellent theology of the Church. What he was saying is that he was a Catholic because he belonged to the local Catholic church of New York. You and I could well say of ourselves something similar to what he said. If, for instance, I were asked: "Are you a *Roman* Catholic?" I could in all truth say: "Well, actually, I'm a Rochester Catholic." (And the reader, having such a question put to her or him, could supply for "Rochester" the name of her or his local church.

In the strictest sense of the term, a *Roman Catholic* is a Catholic who lives in Rome, Italy. If you were to go to Rome, Italy, and ask a person there: "Are you a *Roman Catholic*?," that person could reply in the very strictest sense of the term: "Yes, I am a *Roman Catholic*. I belong to the local church of Rome. The bishop of my local church is John Paul II."

Fellowship (Sisterhood) of Local Churches

Now, lest you misunderstand the point I am trying to make, let me hasten to ask another question: "Is there a true sense in which you and I, who are *Rochester Catholics* (or *New York Catholics* or *Boston Catholics*, etc.) can also be said to be *Roman* Catholics?" The answer, of course, is yes. We are not, it should be clear, *Roman* Catholics in the same sense that Catholics living in Rome are *Roman* Catholics. We are *Roman Catholics* in another, but important sense. We are *Roman Catholics*, because the local church of Rochester (or New York, Boston, etc.) is united with the local church of Rome in a unique way. What does this mean? Simply this: throughout the world there exists a fellowship (or sisterhood, if you prefer) of local churches, to which the local church of Rochester is joined. This fellowship of churches would include the churches of New York, Boston, Chicago, Paris, Montreal, Louisville, Rome, etc. What is it that unites these various churches so that they constitute a true fellowship? It is, among other things, the very important fact that one of these local churches is the center and visible sign of the unity of the churches. And the church that is at the center of Catholic unity is the local church of Rome. The head of the local church of Rome — because this church is at the center — is called the pope, a name that means "Father." The heads of the other local churches throughout the world have authority in their local churches, not as delegates of the pope, but rather as an authority that comes from God. Together with the pope and with him as their leader, they constitute what we call the College of Bishops. It is this college, under the headship of the pope, that has supreme authority in the Church. So, each local bishop has from God the authority to govern and serve his own local church. Together in union with the pope and not apart from him, they share in a concern for the whole church. That is why the Second Vatican Council was so important an event in the life of the contemporary Church. For it brought together in one place all the bishops with the pope as their head.

So, we are *Roman* Catholics, because of our link with other local churches that find their center in the local church of Rome. But — what I want to stress — it is in the local church (whatever local church we belong to) that we experience the reality of Church. It is in the local church that we become conscious of ourselves as "Easter people." For it is in the local church that we are initiated, by baptism, confirmation, and first Eucharist, into the people of God who are the Body of Christ. It is in the local church that the Gospel is proclaimed for us and by us. It is in the local church that we gather as "Easter people," as the family of God, to celebrate the Eucharistic Meal, in which we experience our communion with one another in the Lord Jesus and our ever-growing awareness of God's Presence in our lives.

It is in the context of the local church that we experience the joys and sorrows, the agonies and ecstasies, the certainties and the perplexities that go along with being Christian people on pilgrimage toward the full consummation of what it means to be "Easter people": that final handing over to God when God shall be All in all. It is in the local church that we talk about the things that we believe and strive to live the Gospel values to which we have committed ourselves and discover ever more fully how deeply one with one another we are.

In various local churches and indeed throughout the world there are Catholics who have different views about matters of faith, morality, and spirituality. There are some who believe that the only place from which authentic teaching on these matters can come is the local church of Rome. This seems a difficult position to defend, if we really believe that we are all God's Easter people and that we are all learning from the different experiences we have in living the Gospel in our life's context. Surely, Christians throughout the world, living in different situations and cultures, should be able to say some important things about the way we think and the way we ought to behave and relate ourselves to God. Obviously, the local church of Rome, as the center of unity, could draw on the experiences of the various churches; and, in the light of such collegial involvement, could teach the whole Church in a way that draws on the experiences of all and thus draws all the local churches together.

The Need for Dialogue

One of the problems that we face in the contemporary Church is that the Church of Rome is teaching the whole Church and is not making the effort that many think it should make to be in touch with the way the Gospel truths are being lived and understood in the various local churches throughout the world. Greater consultation and more dialogue are crucial needs in the Church today.

There are a number of areas where such dialogue is needed. We have to talk about how ordinary people in the Church can get a hearing. We must discuss paternalism in the Church and how it has led to a male-dominated Church. How do we right the wrongs of centuries of sexism? Why is it that celibate status has created a privileged class in the Church? How do we create public opinion in the Church? And what is its value? How can such public opinion penetrate the lines of authority that exist in the Church and make itself felt as a movement of the Spirit acting in the whole Church? How do we "evangelize" the notion of authority in the Church and get back to the Gospel understanding of authority as ministry, as service?

All these are "in-house" issues. There are many issues relating the Church to the rest of the world that must also be the subject of dialogue. The Church has to look outside herself and discover, in the light of the Gospel, what role it is called upon to play in the contemporary world: a world of which it is a part, but which in many ways has ceased to take the Church seriously.

As I pointed out earlier in this chapter, no church document has taken more seriously the Church's duty of being involved in the problems and needs of the contemporary world than Vatican II's Pastoral Constitution on the Church in the Modern World (*Gaudium et Spes*). One would search in vain, I think, for an ecclesial document quite like it. First of all, its approach is humble (and need I say that "humble" is not the adjective that generally springs to the mind when one thinks of a church document?): in facing the many problems and needs that beset the contemporary world, it wants to talk, not only to Catholics and to all who invoke the name of Christ, but to the whole of humanity, which it invites to common cause in an enterprise that is for the common good of all. It is humble, too, in that it raises questions for which it has no immediate answers. I don't mean to suggest that the Church has nothing to say to modern issues (it has the all important light of the Gospel to shed on them); what this document makes evident is the willingness on the part of the Church to listen to what others in the human community may have to say. The tone of the document is that, just as the Church has something to say to the modern world, so the world has something to say to the Church. And the document says, in effect: "Tell us what you have to say. We are listening. We want to be partners in dialogue."

Not only is *Gaudium et Spes* a humble document, it is a unique one — and this in a way that is especially pertinent to the theme of this book. For it has let go of the notion, alive for so long a time, that the Church and the world were, almost of necessity, at odds with one another. It is a document that sees the goodness of creation and wants to work with all people of good will to overcome the evils that mar, but can never destroy, that goodness.

Gaudium et Spes articulates *a theological perspective that refuses to separate God from God's creation, as if God were there and creation here.* In terms of the theme of this book, this document signals a rejection of that spiritual apartheid that would separate God from the world, the sacred from the secular and — one almost wants to add in terms of some forms of spirituality — "the holy from the human."

Dialogue — within and without the Church — may well determine how prominent a role the Church will play in the new century that is but a short bit away. There is divine assurance, Christians generally believe, that the Church will survive. There is no such assurance, however, that it will always survive as a significant spiritual, moral, and social force in the years ahead. This depends on the human side of the ecclesial equation. The women and men of the Church have it within themselves to write exclamation points or question marks over different periods of the Church's history. What will the picture be at the beginning of the next century: exclamation point or question mark? Whatever it may be, you and I are beginning the writing of it here and now. The Church that will be is in the making of the Church that is.

A Wider Understanding of Church?

I would like at this point to bring together two ideas, both of which I have already voiced in this book. The first is that there is a *oneness in God* that unites all women and men. This oneness flows from the fact that God is the Hidden Ground of Love of all that is. We are all one in that Ground. The problem that a genuine spirituality must deal with is the fact that we seem to experience separateness rather than oneness. The spiritual life is a journey from the one to the other. *The goal of all true spirituality is to achieve an awareness of our oneness with God and with all of God's creation.* This, clearly, is one of the key ideas of this book.

The second idea, which I want to join to this perception of awareness of unity as the goal of spirituality, is the understanding of Church as "the community of men and women who are aware (in varying degrees of depth) of their oneness with God and with all that is." Juxtaposing these two notions would suggest that it is possible to use the term "Church" in a wider sense than we ordinarily give to the word. If all are one in God (whether they realize it or not), and if awareness of this oneness (with all that it implies) is the goal of human life (whether people realize this or not), is it not possible to say that, in its most universal meaning, "Church" is intended to embrace all of humanity?

To say this is not in any sense to deny the importance of the institutional Church and the unique instrument of grace it can be for us. It is rather to emphasize the (so often unrealized) unity that binds all women and men together, quite apart from their commitment to this or that or to no structured form of religious belief. Indeed, if one looks at the etymology of the word for "Church," both the Greek and the Latin words mean "people called and gathered together by God." If God is the Hidden Ground of Love in which all reality finds its being, uniqueness, and interrelatedness, then it becomes difficult to exclude anyone from the number of those who are thus called.

I am a Roman Catholic and will be eternally grateful to God for the gift of my Catholic faith. At the same time I believe that the divine mercy that brought me to a Roman Catholicism that I have embraced irrevocably has been leading me besides into a world Catholicism. I am discovering that I am more, not less, a Catholic, when I am willing to recognize all the things that God is doing outside the parameters of the institutional structure of which I am, by choice, a part. I can be truly Catholic, not by holding God captive in a single religious tradition (even one to which I am strongly committed), but by realizing that God is above all religious traditions as Savior and Judge of all. God is not, so to put it, a Christian God, in the sense of belonging only to Christian people. God is a Catholic God, that is, a God of all peoples and places, who lives and acts in all, who sustains all by divine love and who leaves traces of the divine Presence in everything that is authentic and genuine in religious rituals, stories, and symbols in whatever part of the world they may be found.

Thomas Merton once wrote to James Baldwin:

> I am...not completely human until I have found myself in my African and Asian and Indonesian brother, because he has the part of humanity that I lack. (*Seeds of Destruction*, p. 305)

In the light of these words of Merton, I put the question (tentatively but genuinely): must I not also say, "I am not completely

Catholic until I have found myself in my Protestant, Jewish, Muslim, Hindu, Buddhist brother and sister; for they have a part of that totality that being Catholic means — which I lack without them"? I am quite aware, as I put this question, that any religion may profess erroneous positions that can mislead a person who is an overardent but poorly informed enthusiast for religious dialogue. True openness to other religions does not mean hasty and uncritical acceptance of what seems to be popular and appealing. It demands, first of all, that I know the rules of good religious dialogue and am firmly grounded in my own faith-tradition. Second, it requires that I sincerely believe that interreligious dialogue can be fruitful. This type of religious openness, in simplest terms, means a willingness to let my own religious tradition be enriched (not replaced) by the religious experiences of a total humanity.

Finally, and ultimately, openness to other religions means that I believe in that most fundamental religious truth (whose depths we so seldom probe) that *God is everywhere* and therefore that wherever we may be — in whatever place, culture, or religion — *we walk in the Presence of the Lord in the land of the living* and experience there *"the Joy of Life in his Presence."*

> *Help me to live*
> *in Your Presence.*

A FOOTNOTE TO CHAPTER TEN:
VARIETY OF MEMBERS IN THE CHURCH

If I were asked to classify the fellow (sister) members of my Church (and classifying people is always a dangerous and often a misleading endeavor), I would be inclined to think of two classes: Catholics who might be called *traditionalists* and Catholics who might be called *prophetic.* The traditionalist Catholics I would, in turn, divide into two groups. By traditionalist Catholics I mean those who want to be faithful to the heritage of faith that has come down to us through the ages from the apostles. They want to preserve continuity with the age of the apostles.

A-historical Traditionalists

One group of traditionalists I would describe as *a-historical*. By this I mean that they believe that the heritage that has come down to us is expressed in unchangeable formulas that are above history, outside of history, and, therefore, untouched by the vagaries and changes that take place in history. They want to keep saying today pretty much the same things that were said in yesteryear. Their attitude: "If the Baltimore Catechism was good enough for me, it's good enough for my children." I don't mean that these people are fanatics. They do see the need for some changes and are willing to accept what they consider reasonable change as good, but — because their view is basically a-historical — they want a minimum of changes. They are uneasy, and even at times disturbed, by the more radical changes advocated by the other group of traditionalists.

Historical Traditionalists

The other group of traditionalists I would mention are people who are equally anxious to preserve the heritage that has come down to us through the ages. But they are *historical* traditionalists. By that I mean that they believe that historical influences affect the way we understand that heritage and there is no possibility of expressing Catholic faith and morals in timeless formulas that can never change.

The categories I have explained may be to some degree oversimplified. But I think you can see the distinction I am trying to make. The a-historical traditionalists see the truths of faith and morals as basically untouched by the historical process, whereas the historical traditionalists feel that our understanding of these truths are strongly affected by history and culture. They would hold that, if truths are wrested out of their historical and cultural context, they lose their intelligibility.

(There is another group of traditionalists I would not want to discuss at any length: they are what I would call *fanatical* traditionalists. These are people who refuse even to discuss change of any kind whatever. They resort to name-calling, accusing those who don't agree with them of being false to Christ and to the Church. They are completely closed to any kind of dialogue. They are getting extensive publicity today, because — unfortunately —

in the present climate of the Church, they are exercising an influence far greater than their numbers warrant.)

Prophetic Voices

Besides the traditionalists, there is another group in the Church, more difficult to describe in a way that will do justice to them. These are those members of the community of "Easter people" who speak in a prophetic way in the midst of the Church. These are the most enigmatic members of the Church — and often the most feared. They "break open" our heritage in such a way that new insights into reality are revealed, new directions for living the Gospel are opened up. What is disturbing about them is that their vision of the Gospel may be so different from that of the rest of Christians that they seem to be advocating not simply change, but a discontinuity with the past and with our Christian beginnings. They seem to be saying things that conflict with ideas, understandings, practices that for so long a time have been cherished by the traditionalists. The prophetic members of the Church are not often popular, especially in their own time. It often is true that it takes time and the perspective of history before we are able to see that the new vision they offered us, which seemed to shatter continuity with the past, comes to be seen as being actually a discovery of that continuity, but at a deeper, more profound level.

I want to conclude this footnote with a warning. Classifying ourselves into various categories or discovering what category I may be in may appear to highlight aspects of our faith-life that divide us. It is important to stress that they are not nearly so important as the single reality that binds us together: namely, the mystery of the death and resurrection of the Lord and all that these realities mean in our lives as individuals and as Church: the coming into full awareness of the Presence of God that is the goal of our existence. What really matters, ultimately, is that "we are Easter people and 'alleluia' is our song."

Conclusion

"Not the intense moment
Isolated, with no before or after,
But a lifetime burning in every moment."
(T. S. Eliot)

A story about St. Teresa of Avila, the authenticity of which I cannot vouch for, has some eager zealot — who was apparently seeking a speedy way to total sanctity — put the following question to this beautiful but very down-to-earth Carmelite nun: "Do you pray well and without distractions?" Her testy retort was: "What do you think I am? A saint?"

This book has been about wordless prayer, though I must admit that I have used a lot of words to describe that which is wordless. What I have tried to discuss is prayer that is not only without words, but without thoughts, images, concepts, concerns, worries, anxieties, and anything else that clutters our minds and hearts; prayer in which we try to empty ourselves, in order that we may be, consciously, full of God. People who have tried to pray in this way are well able to appreciate the response that Avila's most noted citizen gave to her overzealous questioner.

The highest form of this prayer, which transcends words, concepts, images, is contemplation, in which one experiences God in total awareness. Contemplation is not the awareness of God as an Object or of myself as a subject. It is not awareness of *any thing*; it is pure awareness, in which my subjectivity becomes one with the subjectivity of God. My nonseparateness from God as the Hidden Ground of Love of all reality is no longer simply a theological proposition that I assent to; it becomes a personal experience that opens to me a whole new way of looking at reality. I am no longer a victim of spiritual apartheid.

This book is not an attempt to teach people how to become contemplatives (though I have made the point that in the depths of our being we actually are contemplatives, albeit without realizing that we are). I quite readily accept Thomas Merton's remark that one might as easily teach someone how to be an angel as how to be a contemplative. Yet, as Merton also points out, it is possible for us to dispose ourselves for the contemplative experience when it comes. The modest goal of this book is to suggest what I believe is a fruitful way of doing just that: preparing ourselves for contemplation. The way I have suggested is what I have called the "prayer of awareness." Prayer of awareness, as I conceive it, begins with the effort to spend time each day in silence and solitude (however and wherever one may achieve them). This is a time for letting go of all that clutters the mind and the heart — even the good things that are there. It is experiencing our silence as fire: sometimes a warming fire that points the way we must go; sometimes a consuming fire that empties us of all that is not God, so that in emptiness we may be filled with God's fullness.

Because our lives are busy (excessively so for almost all of us), it will not be easy to let go — even for a short time — of all the things that grab for our attention and concern. Distractions will be all too frequent. While they may discourage us, we ought never let them tempt us to give up our prayer. That moment of testing is the time to put to ourselves St. Teresa's question: "What do I think I am? A saint?"

If we persevere in this way of prayer, things will begin to happen in our lives. What starts out as a brief segment of life devoted to "doing prayer" (or, better, "being prayer") becomes, when consistently adhered to, a way of life that affects who we are, what we do, how we think. In the midst of problems, perplexities, difficulties, anxieties (both personal and social), one will find inner peace and silence beginning to grow. Greater gentleness and compassion will mark the way I deal with my sisters and brothers, as awareness deepens of my oneness with them in God. Solidarity with the weak, the vulnerable, the exploited in our society will become a high priority. Above all, I will be more attuned to the grace-filled opportunities of the present moment. I will allow neither backward glances into the past nor tiptoed glimpses into the future to distract my attentiveness to the beauty of what is *now* — that "lifetime burning in every moment." When I look at a flower, I will actually see the flower and see it in God. A Zen writer has put it well:

Silently a flower blooms,
In silence it falls away;
Yet here now, at this moment, at this place
the whole of the flower
the whole of the world is blooming.
This is the talk of the flower, the truth of the blossom;
The glory of eternal life is fully shining here.
(Zenkai Shibayama, *A Flower Does Not Talk*, p. 205)

It may be that somebody is going to put the question to me: "Does this sort of prayer 'work'?" The question could have an ominous tone to it, in case the questioner had in mind a malpractice suit against the author in the event that, after reading the book, he or she discovered that it actually did not "work" and decided to seek redress through legal processes.

All I can hope is that such a questioner would be a person who had not yet read the book. For if he or she had read the book, they would surely realize that what they would be asking is the wrong question. It would be like asking: "Does life work?" or "Does love work?" or "Does truth work?" "Life," "love," and "truth" are not things we *do* to get results. They are realities that in various ways help to define who we are. So "prayer of awareness" is not primarily something we do (in order to achieve certain discernible results), but something we are. We are aware that we are in God. We are aware that we are in Love. Things will happen to us because we are aware, simply because awareness makes us different kinds of persons who inevitably are going to act in new ways. But we do not turn to the prayer of awareness because we want to act in these new ways. In fact we will not achieve any real understanding of these new ways of being and acting till we have arrived at some degree of awareness: awareness of God and of people and the whole wide world in God.

It should be obvious that we have to be serious about this kind of prayer and our commitment to it. Perseverance against whatever odds is imperative. Yet withal we should not be overanxious. We have to avoid the compulsiveness that comes with the desire to "get somewhere" spiritually. That's a wrong kind of goal setting. For, as I have said more than once in this book, we don't have to get anywhere in prayer, because we are already there (in God); we simply have to become aware that we are there.

What is more, the desire to make "progress in the spiritual life," because it concentrates our attention on ourselves and our efforts to realize oneness with God (rather than on God with whom we are one), can be a deterrent to true awareness — as the following story suggests. A zealous young pupil came to his Zen master and asked: "If I really work at it, how long will it take me to achieve enlightenment?" The master's answer was: "If you work *hard* at it, it will take you five years. If you work *very hard*, it will take you twenty years." Or, as the psalmist put it:

> Not to us, Lord, not to us,
> but to your name give glory,
> for your love, for your faithfulness.
> (Ps. 115:1)

Above all, our approach to prayer needs to be simple. For several years now in the city of Rochester, New York, we have been trying to untangle a highway scramble that we have been living with for years. Affectionately dubbed the "Can of Worms," it is at a very busy location and has cars going east and west meeting at the same spot with cars going north and south. With a lot of nerve and a little bit of luck, one can make it through "the Can" unscathed. It would have been so much simpler if it had originally been built as it is now being rebuilt, with east-west traffic on one level and north-south on another.

Sometimes we have to cut through the "can of worms" that we build around our spirituality. The road marked "Awareness" is simple and uncomplicated. We have to leave it that way and let it lead us to that deep consciousness that we are in God and so is everything else that is. This is the goal of life. It is also the beginning of New Life. For it is only when we become who we truly are that we begin really to live. We live fully in the here and now, experiencing "a lifetime burning in every moment."